OECD *Economic Surveys*
Electronic Books

The OECD, recognising the strategic role of electronic publishing, will be issuing the OECD *Economic Surveys*, both for the Member countries and for countries of Central and Eastern Europe covered by the Organisation's Centre for Co-operation with Economies in Transition, as electronic books with effect from the 1994/1995 series -- incorporating the text, tables and figures of the printed version. The information will appear on screen in an identical format, including the use of colour in graphs.

The electronic book, which retains the quality and readability of the printed version throughout, will enable readers to take advantage of the new tools that the ACROBAT software (included on the diskette) provides by offering the following benefits:

❑ User-friendly and intuitive interface
❑ Comprehensive index for rapid text retrieval, including a table of contents, as well as a list of numbered tables and figures
❑ Rapid browse and search facilities
❑ Zoom facility for magnifying graphics or for increasing page size for easy readability
❑ Cut and paste capabilities
❑ Printing facility
❑ Reduced volume for easy filing/portability

Working environment: DOS, Windows or Macintosh.

Subscription: FF 1 800   US$317   £200   DM 545

Single issue: FF 130   US$24   £14   DM 40

Complete 1994/1995 series on CD-ROM:

FF 2 000   US$365   £220   DM 600

Please send your order to OECD Electronic Editions or, preferably, to the Centre or bookshop with whom you placed your initial order for this Economic Survey.

OECD
ECONOMIC
SURVEYS

1994-1995

NORWAY

ORGANISATION FOR ECONOMIC CO-OPERATION AND DEVELOPMENT

ORGANISATION FOR ECONOMIC CO-OPERATION AND DEVELOPMENT

Pursuant to Article 1 of the Convention signed in Paris on 14th December 1960, and which came into force on 30th September 1961, the Organisation for Economic Co-operation and Development (OECD) shall promote policies designed:

- to achieve the highest sustainable economic growth and employment and a rising standard of living in Member countries, while maintaining financial stability, and thus to contribute to the development of the world economy;
- to contribute to sound economic expansion in Member as well as non-member countries in the process of economic development; and
- to contribute to the expansion of world trade on a multilateral, non-discriminatory basis in accordance with international obligations.

The original Member countries of the OECD are Austria, Belgium, Canada, Denmark, France, Germany, Greece, Iceland, Ireland, Italy, Luxembourg, the Netherlands, Norway, Portugal, Spain, Sweden, Switzerland, Turkey, the United Kingdom and the United States. The following countries became Members subsequently through accession at the dates indicated hereafter: Japan (28th April 1964), Finland (28th January 1969), Australia (7th June 1971), New Zealand (29th May 1973) and Mexico (18th May 1994). The Commission of the European Communities takes part in the work of the OECD (Article 13 of the OECD Convention).

Publié également en français.

Table of contents

Boxes

Tables

Figures

BASIC STATISTICS OF NORWAY

THE LAND

Area (1 000 sq. km)	324	Major cities (1.1.94)	
Agricultural area (1 000 sq. km)	9	Oslo	477 515
Productive forests (1 000 sq. km)	65	Bergen	219 810

THE PEOPLE

Population, (31.12.1993)	4 324 577	Civilian employment, 1993	1 970 000
Number of inhabitants per sq. km	13	*of which:*	
Net natural increase		Industry (%)	23.1
(average 1989-1992)	15 073	Agriculture, forestry and fishing (%)	5.6
Per 1 000 inhabitants	3.5	Other activities (%)	71.3
(average 1989-92)			

PRODUCTION

Gross domestic product, 1994	774 244	Gross fixed capital investment (1994):	
(NKr million)		Percentage of GDP	18.3
GDP per head (1994, US$)	25 409	Per head, US$	4 653

THE GOVERNMENT

Public consumption in 1993		Composition of Parliament (number of seats):	
(percentage of GDP)	22.0	Labour Party	67
General government current and capital		Conservative Party	28
expenditure in 1993 (percentage of GDP)	57.0	Christian Democratic Party	13
General government revenue in 1993		Centre (Agrarian Party)	32
(percentage of GDP)	54.3	Progress Party	10
		Social Left Party	13
		Others	2
		Total	165
Last general elections: 1993		Next general elections: 1997	

FOREIGN TRADE

Exports of goods and services		Imports of goods and services	
(average 1989-1994, as a per cent of GDP)	43.5	(average 1989-94, as a per cent of GDP)	39.6
of which:		Main imports in 1994 (percentage of total	
Gross freight and oil drilling (1989-94)	6.7	commodity imports):	
Main exports in 1994 (percentage of total		Ships	4.0
commodity exports):		Machinery, apparatus and transport	
Forestry products	3.8	equipment (excluding ships)	31.6
Base metals and products thereof	11.4	Raw materials (non-edible), including	
Fish and fish products	7.7	fuel and chemicals	13.4
Machinery, apparatus and transport		Base metals and products thereof	11.0
equipment (excluding ships)	8.3		

THE CURRENCY

Monetary unit: Krone		Currency units per US$, average of daily	
		figures:	
		Year 1994	7.06
		June 1995	6.23

Note: An international comparison of certain basic statistics is given in an annex table.

This Survey is based on the Secretariat's study prepared for the annual review of Norway by the Economic and Development Review Committee on 19 June 1995.

•

After revisions in the light of discussions during the review, final approval of the Survey for publication was given by the Committee on 10 July 1995.

•

The previous Survey of Norway was issued in March 1994.

Introduction

The recovery of the Norwegian economy gathered momentum in 1994, reflecting continued buoyancy in household spending and a pick up in international demand for traditional mainland exports. In the course of the year, the upturn also spread to mainland capital formation. With overall real GDP growth (including oil) exceeding 5 per cent, private sector employment rose for the first time since 1987, helping to reduce the unemployment rate by one point from its peak of 6½ per cent in mid-1993. Wage and price inflation has remained moderate, however, with the annual average rate of consumer price increases since 1992 staying below 2 per cent. At the same time, the improved export performance and reduced external debt servicing have led to a widening of the external surplus.

Projections by the OECD point to a continuation of the recovery through 1996, though at a slower pace. Economic activity should be spurred by strong growth in mainland business investment as corporate profitability has improved and spare capacity is being exhausted. By contrast, capital formation on the Norwegian Continental Shelf is expected to be less buoyant. Household spending is also projected to grow less vigorously than in the recent past, with most pent-up demand now satisfied, following the sharp reduction in personal debt accumulated in the 1980s. The labour market situation could become tighter, which might culminate in accelerated wage growth next year and possible inflation pressures. Production of oil and gas should again increase rapidly, boosting overall GDP growth and adding to the already substantial current account surplus.

The mix of macroeconomic policies has been fundamentally altered since the early 1990s. The strength of the exchange rate since the floating of the Norwegian Krone in December 1992 allowed a marked decline in interest rates, which facilitated the recovery of domestic demand. By contrast, fiscal policy has become progressively more restrictive, with the general government budget balance moving towards surpluses. While contributing to support monetary policy in keeping inflation under control, the improved budget position should help reduce the strains that the expected fall in petroleum revenues and increase in public pension payments will put on the budget in the next decades.

Chapter I of the *Survey* briefly examines trends since early 1994 and discusses the short-term prospects. This is followed by a review of macroeconomic policies in Chapter II and of recent progress in structural reform in Chapter III. Chapter IV provides a detailed analysis of the long-run constraints on fiscal policy associated with future developments in oil income and the ageing of the population. Conclusions of the *Survey* are presented in Chapter V.

I. Recent developments and short-term prospects

A stronger and broader recovery

The recovery of mainland activity, which started in 1992, gathered momentum during the second half of 1993 and in 1994. Mainland economic growth indeed accelerated from around 2 per cent in 1993 to a twenty-year high of nearly 4 per cent in 1994, reducing the output gap from 4 per cent in late-1992 to about 1 per cent by the end of last year (Figure 1). New extraction capacity on the Norwegian Continental Shelf has boosted oil and gas production, raising overall (mainland and offshore) GDP growth to 2.4 per cent in 1993 and 5.1 per cent in 1994. These developments were reflected in improved labour market conditions, while inflation has remained broadly stable.

The main impulses came from buoyancy in household spending – triggered by a significant easing of monetary conditions – and a pickup in traditional exports (Table 1). Further impetus originated from surging investment deliveries to the offshore sector and, more recently, increased capital formation in the non-oil business sector in response to improved profitability and faster output growth. The paragraphs below describe in more detail these main features of the upturn.

Still buoyant oil activity

The resilience in the oil and gas sector observed since the late 1980s has become more marked in recent years. Oil and gas production surged by 6 per cent in 1993 and 12 per cent in 1994, adding in these years 0.9 and 1.8 percentage points, respectively, to overall GDP growth. The bulk of this production being sold abroad, petroleum exports expanded by 6 per cent in 1993 and 11 per cent in 1994. Moreover, after several years of unabated expansion of extraction capacity

3

Figure 1. **GROWTH PERFORMANCE**

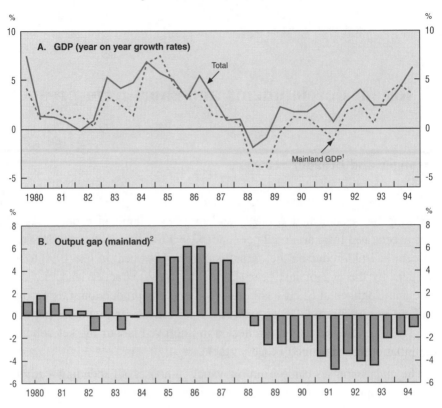

1. Mainland GDP excludes North Sea production, oil platforms and ships.
2. The gap between actual and trend mainland GDP as a percentage of trend mainland GDP.
Source: OECD, *Quarterly National Accounts,* Secretariat estimates.

on the Norwegian Continental Shelf, offshore investments (including platforms under construction) attained a new historical peak of NKr 56 billion or over 7 per cent of GDP in 1994. Such buoyant petroleum activity has also affected business in the mainland economy. Indeed, with approximately half of the construction work carried out domestically, the increased investment on the Norwegian Continental Shelf appears to have raised mainland GDP by roughly 1 1/2 per cent in the 1992-94 period.

4

Table 1. **Demand and output**

Percentage changes from previous period, seasonally adjusted at annual rates, volume

	1991 current prices NKr billion	1992	1993	1994	1993 2nd half	1994 1st half	1994 2nd half
Private consumption	349.7	1.8	2.3	4.4	7.2	3.9	2.7
Government consumption	147.5	4.4	1.8	2.7	7.3	3.0	-1.4
Gross fixed capital formation[1]	136.8	-0.5	4.7	4.8	18.3	-6.5	15.3
of which:							
Oil sector[1]	41.3	8.6	15.9	1.8	22.5	-12.5	15.6
Residential	14.1	-12.6	-5.2	33.8	21.6	37.8	37.4
Other business	51.3	4.7	-1.0[2]	4.8	15.5	-13.4	34.2
Government	24.3	5.3	-11.6[2]	-4.7	1.0	-13.7	7.0
Stockbuilding[3]	-7.7	-0.2	0.4	0.5	–	–	–
Total domestic demand	626.3	1.7	3.2	4.7	11.5	2.1	3.9
Exports	307.5	6.2	1.6	7.6	6.1	9.5	5.6
of which:							
Oil and gas	96.7	10.8	5.8	11.2	12.8	16.1	0.8
Goods (excluding ships)	112.5	4.1	3.0	14.3	6.5	17.4	16.3
Imports	247.1	2.8	3.2	7.2	15.0	2.4	10.0
of which: Mainland goods	152.1	3.9	1.8	14.9	18.1	15.1	12.0
GDP	686.7	3.4	2.4	5.1	7.8	5.3	2.5
Memorandum items:							
Mainland GDP	563.8	2.1	2.1	3.9	5.0	4.4	2.3
OECD Europe GDP	–	1.6	-0.1	2.4	1.5	2.9	2.7

1. Including platforms under construction.
2. Growth rates for other business sector and government investment are heavily affected by administrative changes which occurred in the ownership structure of buildings used by the state.
3. Contribution to GDP growth, excluding platforms under construction.
Source: OECD.

Surge in household demand

After several years of stagnation, both private consumption and residential investment picked up sharply in the second half of 1993, and continued to expand rapidly during 1994 (Table 1). This reflected significant progress in households' financial consolidation and the rapid fall in interest rates as from early 1993. Indeed, the brisk improvement in households' net asset position (Figure 2) appears to have released pent-up demand accumulated while their balance sheets

Figure 2. **PROGRESS IN HOUSEHOLD FINANCIAL CONSOLIDATION**

Per cent of disposable income

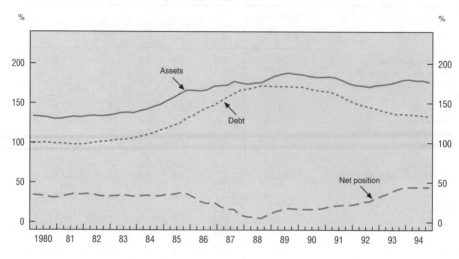

Source: Bank of Norway.

Table 2. **Household appropriation account**

Percentage change from previous year

	1991	1992	1993	1994
Real consumption expenditure	0.0	1.8	2.3	4.4
Real disposable income	1.7	4.6	2.6	2.2
Contribution from:				
Wages	0.2	0.5	0.9	2.9
Profit income	−0.4	0.3	0.9	0.9
Net public transfers	1.9	1.7	0.8	0.1
Net interest payments, etc.	0.1	1.5	1.1	0.1
Direct taxes [1]	0.0	0.7	−1.2	−1.7
Saving ratio, level in per cent	2.6	5.2	5.5	3.4
Memorandum item:				
Private consumption deflator	4.1	2.6	1.9	1.4

1. A positive contribution implies that *real* direct taxes have been reduced. Does not include changes in social security tax paid by employers.
Source: Statistics Norway.

6

were being restructured. In addition, households' confidence has been strengthened by a more rapid expansion in real disposable income, with increases in wage and entrepreneurial income more than offsetting reduced growth in income transfers (Table 2).

The turnaround in private demand has been most pronounced for consumer durables, private cars in particular (Figure 3, Panels A and B). The housing market has also become more buoyant: following a long period of decline, house prices started to recover in early 1993 (Figure 3, Panel C), pushing up housing starts by 75 per cent (s.a.) between the second quarter of 1993 and the fourth quarter of 1994. This was reflected in a steep pickup in residential investment by more than 30 per cent in 1994 (Figure 3, Panel D).

Rising mainland business investment

With slack in the mainland business sector progressively removed, mainland business investment picked up in the course of 1994, growing by almost 34 per cent (seasonally-adjusted annual rate) in the second half. The upturn of investment has been most marked in the service sector, which has benefited from the acceleration in household spending in 1993 (Figure 4, Panels A and B). Manufacturing investment, however, is likely to follow suit quickly, as a surge in international commodity prices has boosted profitability in this sector. Indeed, rates of return on capital in manufacturing are estimated to have recovered strongly in 1993 and 1994 to levels slightly above the average for the 1980s.[1] Thus, there appears to be ample scope for further investment growth, with the ratio of investment to value added and the capital/output ratio both below their historical trends (Figure 4, Panels C and D).

Improved labour market conditions

The strengthening of private sector activity has substantially reduced slack in the labour market. For the first time since 1987, private sector (and total) employment increased in 1994. This contributed to a decline in the rate of "open" unemployment (i.e. excluding participants in labour market

7

Figure 3. **HOUSEHOLD DEMAND**

Q1 1980 = 100, seasonally adjusted

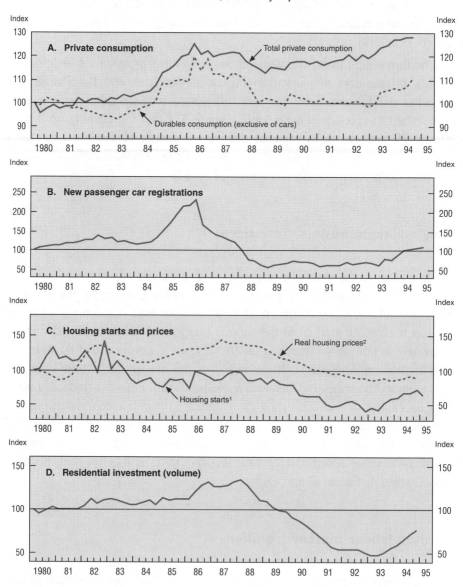

1. Thousands, monthly averages.
2. New dwellings. Deflated by the private consumption deflator.
Source: OECD, *Quarterly National Accounts, Main Economic Indicators.*

8

Figure 4. **MAINLAND BUSINESS INVESTMENT**

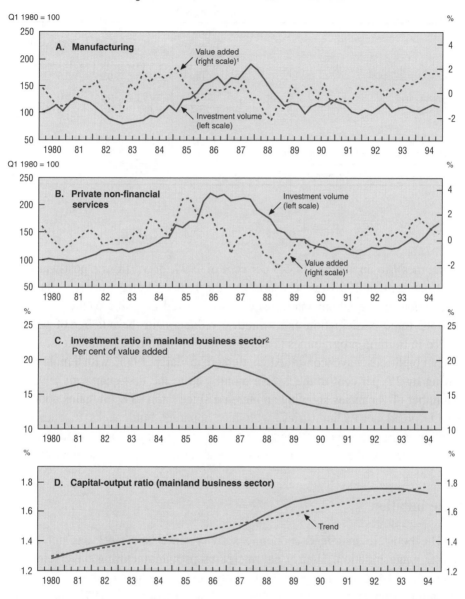

1. Per cent change over 4 quarters, 3 quarters moving average.
2. Excluding residential "sector", petroleum production and shipping. The figures are calculated as investment divided by value added in the sector.
Source: OECD, *National Accounts.*

Table 3. **Labour market developments**

Per cent change from previous year

	1990 Thousand persons	1991	1992	1993	1994
Labour force	2 144	−0.7	0.2	0.0	0.9
Employment, total	2 032	−0.9	−0.2	0.0	1.5
Public sector	567	2.9	3.2	2.6	1.9
Private	1 464	−2.3	−1.6	−1.1	1.4
Unemployment	112	3.6	8.6	0.8	−8.7
Level, as a percentage of the labour force	−	5.5	5.9	6.0	5.4

Source: Statistics Norway, Labour Market Surveys and Ministry of Finance.

programmes)[2] to an average of 5.5 per cent in 1994, down from a post-war peak of 6.0 per cent in 1993 (as measured by the Labour Force Survey).[3] Such an improvement in the labour market situation occurred despite a cyclical rebound of labour force participation and a modest reduction in the number of persons enrolled in training programmes (Table 3). According to recent indicators, labour market conditions have continued to tighten in early 1995, with employment growing by 2½ per cent in the twelve months up to the first quarter of 1995 and the number of vacancies showing an increase since late 1994. Job gains appear to be widespread across industries, with few apparent bottlenecks to date – an exception being the construction sector, which has been affected by the surge in investment in dwellings and structures (including a new airport near Oslo).

Stable inflation

The boost in mainland economic activity since mid-1993 has not led to stronger wage inflation. Hourly pay increases in manufacturing have remained modest since 1992, in a range of 2½ to 3 per cent per annum (Table 4). Ongoing negotiations suggest that wage increases will stay moderate in 1995. Indeed, for the time being, the Confederation of Labour Unions is still supporting wage moderation so as not to put the external competitiveness of the mainland economy at risk. Unit labour costs have thus developed favourably – both in manufac-

Table 4. **Prices, wages and costs**

Percentage change from previous year

	1991	1992	1993	1994
Consumer prices	3.4	2.3	2.3	1.4
Imported consumer goods	2.0	1.8	3.3	2.3
Hourly wages:				
Manufacturing	5.3	3.4	2.8	2.7
Private sector	5.2	2.8	2.8	2.9
Hourly compensation per employee				
Mainland economy	5.1	2.8	0.8	2.8
Manufacturing	4.7	2.8	0.9	2.7
Unit labour costs				
Mainland economy	4.2	1.1	–0.5	0.5
Manufacturing	3.9	1.0	–1.1	1.6

Source: Statistics Norway.

turing and in the economy as a whole – and have remained practically unchanged in the wake of the protracted economic slack of the years 1988-92, before edging up in late 1994. These developments have been helped by a fall in non-wage labour costs in 1993 when employers' social security contributions were cut.

The virtual stability in unit wage costs has been one of the main factors underpinning the persistence of low consumer price inflation since early 1992, with the year-on-year increase in the consumer price index (CPI) ranging between 1 and 2½ per cent (Figure 5, Panel A). Although Norway's inflation performance has been favourable in recent years compared with its main trading partners, this outcome needs to be assessed against the substantial slack in the mainland economy in the period 1988-92, which implied stronger downward pressure on profit margins and wage settlements than elsewhere (Figure 5, Panel B). In 1994 and in early 1995, however, signs of rising inflation have emerged – with year-on-year price increases approaching 2¾ per cent in February 1995. Such a development is mainly attributable to the indirect tax increases implemented in mid-1994 and early 1995. As measured by the Bank of Norway, the underlying rate of inflation (corrected for the effects of administered prices, indirect taxes and change in housing rents) has drifted up from some 1½ per cent in the second quarter of 1994 to just over 2 per cent in the first

Figure 5. **INFLATION PERFORMANCE**

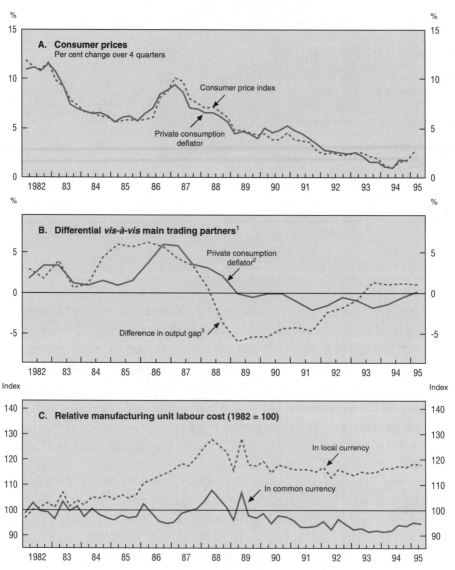

1. Norway minus partners: Great Britain, Sweden, Germany, Netherlands, France, United States, Denmark, Finland, Italy, Canada, Japan, Spain.
2. Per cent change over 4 quarters.
3. Defined as the norwegian output gap (mainland) minus the weighted output gap of main trading partners.
Source: OECD, *Main Economic Indicators, National Accounts.*

12

quarter of 1995. As noted, relative unit labour costs in manufacturing – both measured in local currencies and after correction for movements in exchange rates (Figure 5, Panel C) – also increased at the end of 1994, reversing the downward trend that started in 1988.

Continued large external surplus

The current account balance has now been positive for six consecutive years, with the surplus increasing from 2.1 per cent of GDP in 1993 to 3.3 per cent in 1994 (Figure 6, Panel A). This outcome is largely attributable to a rising surplus on the offshore trade balance and a decline in the deficit on the invest-ment-income account. The latter owes to a rapid reduction in net foreign debt – from 22.5 per cent of GDP in 1988 to 3 per cent in 1994 – and an associated fall in debt servicing costs (Figure 7). In addition, with the impact of the tax reform of 1992 waning, repatriation of profits of foreign enterprises engaged in Norway's offshore industry has fallen back to normal levels. The surplus on the "offshore" trade balance rose from an already comfortable 12 per cent of GDP in 1993 to 14 per cent in 1994 (Figure 6, Panel C), as the surge in petroleum output more than offset the effect of the falling oil price (from an average of NKr 123 per barrel in 1993 to NKr 111 last year).

By contrast, after a favourable development in 1993, the "traditional" trade deficit deteriorated from its 1993 level of 6.2 per cent of GDP to 6.7 per cent in 1994 (Figure 6, Panel B). This occurred despite a surge in manufacturing exports in 1994 by 14 per cent, after a 3 per cent growth rate recorded for 1993. Such a good export performance reflects both the rapid expansion in the world market for manufacturing products (from 1 per cent in 1993 to 10 per cent in 1994, as weighted according to the geographical destinations of Norwegian exports) and a shift of international demand from finished products towards processed raw materials (which are predominant in Norwegian manufacturing exports). Due to the pickup in domestic demand in Norway, however, growth of imports of goods has also been strong, accelerating from 1.8 per cent in 1993 to 15 per cent in 1994.

Figure 6. **THE CURRENT BALANCE AND ITS MAJOR COMPONENTS**

As a percentage of GDP

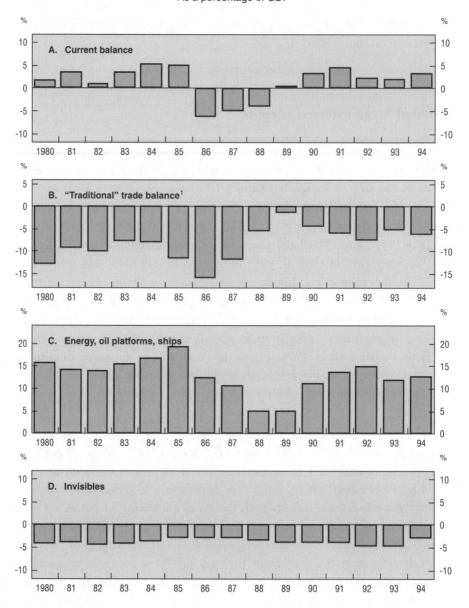

1. Excluding exports and imports of petroleum, oil rigs and ships.
Source: Statistics Norway.

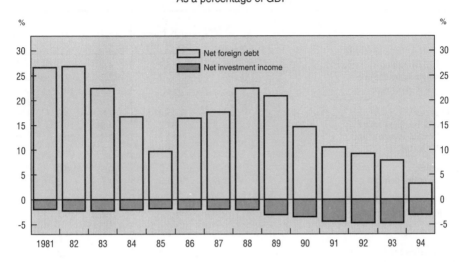

Figure 7. **NET FOREIGN DEBT AND INVESTMENT INCOME**
As a percentage of GDP

Short-term outlook

While slowing, the recovery is projected to continue, with mainland GDP expanding by nearly 3 per cent in 1995 and 2½ per cent next year (Table 5). Including oil activity, overall GDP growth is expected to be again somewhat stronger. Growth in household spending may be less buoyant than in 1994, as the impact of monetary easing is expected to wane. As well, capital formation on the Norwegian Continental Shelf is likely to fall, partly offset by resilience in mainland business investment which is spurred by improved profitability and high capacity utilisation. Traditional exports may slow down in line with projected market growth. With offshore exports remaining strong, the current account surplus is expected to keep rising, also underpinned by a further improved investment-income balance.

While employment growth is envisaged to be strong, the reduction in unemployment may be tempered by a further rebound of labour force participation and a drop in the number of persons enrolled in active labour market programmes. Wage growth, nonetheless, is projected to accelerate towards the end of the

15

Table 5. **Short-term projections**[1]

Percentage changes, volume

	1992 current prices NKr billion	1994	1995	1996
Private consumption	365.2	4.4	2.9	2.5
Government consumption	157.2	2.7	1.2	1.0
Gross fixed investment[2]	138.7	4.8	10.1	−3.1
of which:				
Oil sector[2]	45.2	1.8	4.0	−20.0
Non-oil business sector	54.2	4.8	19.9	7.8
Residential construction	12.3	33.8	20.0	10.0
Public sector	25.6	−4.8	−4.0	0.9
Stockbuilding[3]	−9.2	0.5	0.0	0.0
Total domestic demand	651.8	4.7	4.2	0.8
Exports of goods and services	303.2	7.6	8.2	6.1
of which: Energy exports	–	11.2	10.2	8.5
Imports of goods and services	252.0	7.2	7.3	0.0
Foreign balance[4]	51.2	0.9	1.2	3.0
GDP	703.0	5.1	4.8	3.5
Mainland GDP	584.8	3.9	2.9	2.5
Memorandum items:				
Mainland GDP deflator	–	2.1	2.7	2.4
Private consumption deflator	–	1.4	2.8	2.6
Employment	–	1.5	1.4	1.2
Unemployment rate	–	5.4	4.9	4.5
Private compensation per employee	–	3.1	3.3	3.8

1. Projections published in the OECD *Economic Outlook 57*, July 1995.
2. Includes platforms under construction.
3. Contribution to GDP growth, excluding platforms under construction.
4. Contribution to GDP growth.
Source: OECD.

projection period to nearly 4 per cent in response to improved corporate profitability and the better labour market conditions. Such wage increases would still be relatively moderate given the expected strength of the economy. Indeed, according to simulations with national models,[4] a wage growth of around 5 to 5¹/₂ per cent in 1996 would be broadly consistent with the projected fall in unemployment. Assuming that social partners will be willing to support wage moderation to a greater extent than in previous cycles, consumer price inflation is projected to remain stable at its early 1995 rate of 2½ per cent. The recent appreciation of the currency and the waning impact of the earlier indirect tax increases should also help to maintain price stability.

These projections, which are consistent with those published in *Economic Outlook No. 57* (June 1995), are based upon the following main assumptions:

– the predicted growth pattern in the OECD area should lead Norwegian manufacturing export markets to grow by 9½ and 7½ per cent in 1995 and 1996 respectively;
– the average OECD oil-import price is expected to recover somewhat from US$14.6 in 1994 to US$16.7 in 1995 and US$17 in 1996;
– a modest tightening of monetary conditions in Europe in early 1996 is assumed to be followed by Norwegian monetary authorities to pre-empt inflationary pressures and keep the ECU exchange rate roughly unchanged at its May 1995 level. However, long-term rates are expected to decline slightly from their current level, in line with German rates;
– government expenditure is assumed to increase at rates significantly below the trend for mainland GDP in both 1995 and 1996, while main-land tax ratios are kept unchanged from those implied by the 1995 Revised Budget. According to estimates by the OECD, this would result in a reduction in the structural non-oil budget deficit from 6.5 per cent of mainland GDP in 1994 to 5.1 per cent in 1995 and 4.4 per cent in 1996.

There are a number of risks attached to this projection. First, if domestic demand growth does not subside as projected, bottlenecks in the economy could arise and stronger inflationary pressures would emerge, in which case cost com-petitiveness might be eroded. In addition, an unexpected rise in oil prices – not excluded in view of the global recovery – could lead to a larger government budget surplus than projected (see Chapter II) and, consequently, raise pressures for higher public spending. If these pressures materialised, the risk of economic overheating and higher inflation would be heightened.

II. Macroeconomic policies

The mix of macroeconomic policies has significantly changed since the early 1990s, with monetary conditions easing in the wake of the floating of the currency in December 1992 while the fiscal stance moved towards restriction. Such a reorientation of policy instruments has provided strong impetus to mainland economic growth, as reflected in the progressive narrowing of the output gap (Figure 8). This is in line with the Long-Term Programme 1994-97 presented to the Parliament in February 1993, which emphasised that durable non-inflationary growth would require a combination of fiscal consolidation and credible mone-

Figure 8. **THE POLICY MIX OVER THE BUSINESS CYCLE**

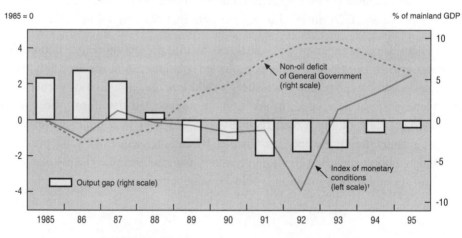

1. Index constructed by the Bank of Norway using a weighted average of changes in the real 3-month money market (2/3) and real effective exchange rates (1/3). An increase in the index points to an easing of monetary conditions.
Source: 1995 National Budget; Bank of Norway, *Penger Og Kreditt;* OECD Secretariat.

tary policy geared towards long-run price stability. The government's commitment to such a strategy will be tested in the coming years, with the ongoing recovery entering a phase where inflation may accelerate, at a time when rising fiscal surpluses – partly due to the buoyant petroleum sector – could lead to pressure for increased public spending.

Monetary management

The policy formulation

The decision by the Norwegian monetary authorities to let the krone float in response to the turmoil in European exchange markets in late 1992 has not fundamentally changed the conduct of monetary policy. This has remained geared towards price stability through the maintenance of a stable exchange rate *vis-à-vis* countries pursuing low-inflation objectives. Such an orientation was reinforced by the adoption of a new monetary-policy framework in May 1994, legally committing the Bank of Norway to focus on the "stability in the value of the krone as measured against European currencies" at the level which had been prevailing subsequent to the floating in December 1992, which was about 3 to 5 per cent below the pre-floating ECU parity. Although intervention margins have not been established, short-term deviations from this target range seem generally to have been counteracted.

Two main reasons justify the priority attached to the exchange rate as a guide for monetary policy. First, in a small open economy like Norway, with a very high import content of domestic demand, the stability in the external value of the currency is seen as a prerequisite for keeping inflation under control. In light of past experience, exchange rate depreciation could indeed weaken wage discipline and, in turn, generate inflation pressure. Second, volatility in the krone's exchange rate is regarded as potentially damaging to domestic manufacturing industries, as these are widely exposed to international competition.

So far financial markets have shown confidence in the ability of monetary policy, as currently formulated, to keep inflation under control. This is reflected in the behaviour of long term interest rates, which have been broadly declining since late 1992. Such confidence of the financial community is justified by the country's strong economic fundamentals, including a rising external surplus, a projected surplus of general government and continued low inflation. However, the real test for monetary policy will come in the years ahead if inflation pressures re-emerge with the slack in the economy gradually shrinking. This could confront the monetary authorities with the dilemma of either raising interest rates to prevent price increases from accelerating (though this could lead to upward pressure on the krone), or giving priority to exchange rate stability – with the risk that a delay in monetary tightening would undermine confidence in the authorities' commitment to price stability.

Exchange and interest rate developments

Since December 1992 the Norwegian krone has remained relatively stable, within a range of 3 to 5 per cent below its pre-floating parity against the ECU (Figure 9, Panel A). In wider trade-weighted terms the krone has been somewhat more volatile, but strengthened on average in the last two years due mainly to the weakening of the dollar. The krone's performance is particularly impressive when compared with other currencies that have been floating since 1992 (Figure 9, Panel B), which reflects the strong fundamentals of Norway relative to the economies concerned, Sweden in particular. The strength of the krone allowed the monetary authorities to use the massive capital inflows subsequent to the floating to replenish foreign currency reserves, which had been depleted by the support operations in the second half of 1992. Since mid-1993 spot interventions by the Bank of Norway have been quite small, though, with the bulk taking place in the weeks up to the EU referendum on 28 November to dampen the volatility of the currency in that period (Figure 9, Panel C).

Heightened confidence in the krone and a fall in interest rates across Europe permitted substantial reductions in Norwegian short term interest rates between late 1992 and early 1994, with the three-month money market rate declining from a peak of 16 per cent in November 1992 to 5½ per cent in February 1994. At the same time, official short-term rates were cut by almost the same amount (Figure 10, Panel A). As a result, short-term interest differentials with Germany had been eliminated by early 1993, and were negative for the rest of the year and the beginning of 1994 (Figure 10, Panel B). The differential turned positive again in the run-up to the EU referendum in late November, when the three-month rate climbed to a 1994-peak of just over 7 per cent. However, this rise had been

Figure 9. **EXCHANGE RATE BEHAVIOUR
AND OFFICIAL RESERVES**

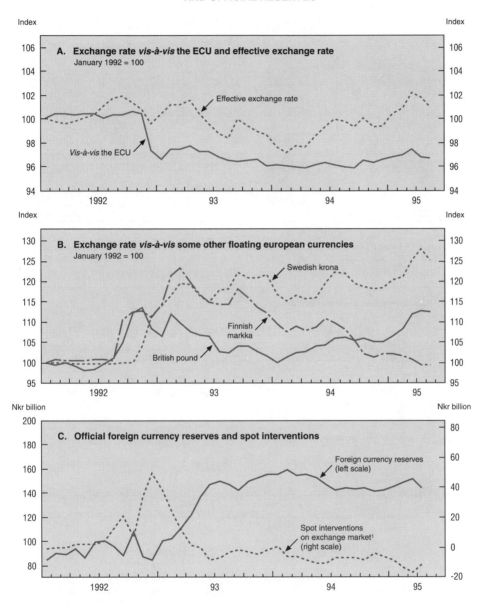

1.   Net accumulated sales of currency to banks from January 1992 onwards.
Source: Bank of Norway; Statistics Norway.

Figure 10. **INTEREST RATE DEVELOPMENTS**

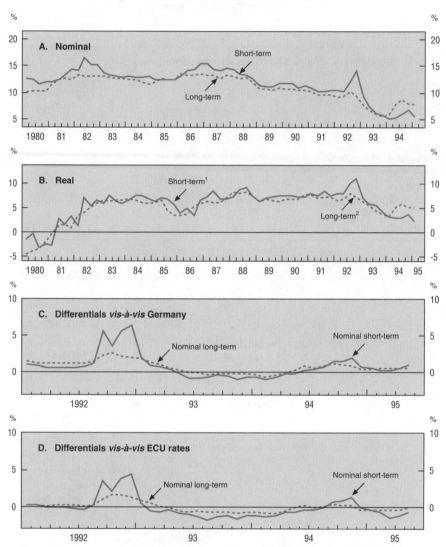

1. 3-month Nibor rate less the expected rate of inflation, the latter being measured by the percentage change in the CPI (at annual rate) over the quarter preceding and the two quarters following each observation.
2. Yield of long-term government bonds less the expected rate of inflation, the latter being measured by the percentage change in the CPI over the 4 quarters following each observation.
   From first quarter of 1995 to fourth quarter of 1995, OECD projections for the CPI are used.
Source: IMF, *International Financial Statistics;* OECD, *Main Economic Indicators.*

mostly reversed by April 1995, with the short-term rate back at 5½ per cent, some 100 basis points above the equivalent German rate.[5] Short-term interest rates are currently at their lowest levels since 1980, both in nominal and real terms.

Long-term rates, as well, have fallen markedly since the floating, the yield on government bonds with a six to ten-year maturity reaching a fifteen-year low of 5¾ per cent in February 1994. The subsequent increase – to 8 per cent in March 1995 – is essentially due to the global rise in long-term rates across the OECD area. Overall, however, the differential *vis-à-vis* Germany has remained largely unchanged since early 1993, with a temporary upward move during the run-up to the EU referendum in the autumn of 1994. It has subsequently declined to 0.6 percentage points.

Improved bank profitability and resumption of credit growth

The banking crisis of the early 1990s[6] – which led the government to inject substantial capital (some 3 per cent of GDP over 1991-1993) in the major financial institutions – came to an end by 1993. In 1994 both commercial and savings banks reported operating profits at or above the average levels that prevailed in the first half of the 1980s, helped by a strong reduction in provisions against loan losses (Figure 11, Panels A and B), and despite losses on bond portfolios following the rise in long-term interest rates (Table 6). Improved bank profitability was mirrored by a steep fall in the number of bankruptcies (Figure 11, Panel C). Savings banks, in particular, have benefited from a continued decline in operating costs – from 3.5 per cent of average assets in 1991 to 2.9 per cent in 1994 – owing to rationalisation efforts, culminating in reduced staff and branch numbers (see below).

These developments have led to a significant strengthening of the capital base in the banking industry: by the end of 1994, the capital adequacy ratios of savings banks and, to a lesser extent, of commercial banks had risen to levels well above the minima required by the BIS since 1991. This reflects banks' efforts to boost their creditworthiness in order to reduce funding costs and, in turn, price loans more competitively without making inroads into lending margins, which have been under downward pressure for some years. Indeed, as shown in Figure 12, the spread between long-term lending rates and rates on time deposits declined from just over 5 per cent in 1989 to 3½ per cent in 1994. In part, such a reduction in banks' lending margins at the long end is due to

23

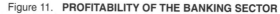

Figure 11. **PROFITABILITY OF THE BANKING SECTOR**

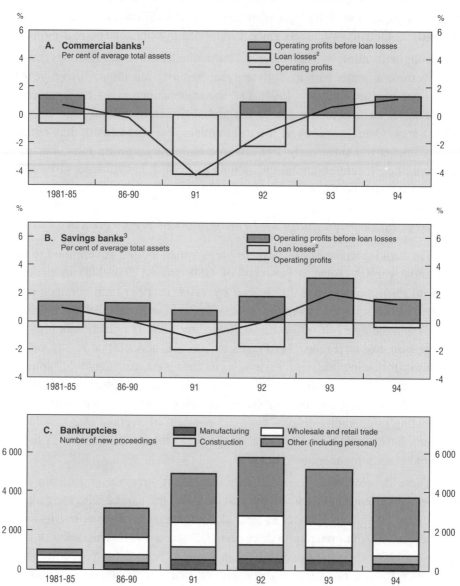

1. Parent banks.
2. Includes losses resulting from bank guarantees.
3. 24 largest banks for the period 1991-92, 30 largest banks for the period 1993-94.
Source: Statistics Norway; Bank of Norway; OECD Secretariat.

Table 6. **Banks' operating results**

Per cent of annual average total assets

	Averages		1991	1992	1993	1994
	1981-85	1986-90				
Commercial banks [1]						
Net interest revenues	3.3	2.8	2.5	2.9	3.1	2.8
Other operating revenues	1.4	1.2	0.9	1.1	1.5	1.0
Operating costs [2]	3.3	2.8	3.3	2.9	2.5	2.5
Operating profits before losses	1.4	1.2	0.0	1.0	2.0	1.4
Loan losses [3]	0.7	1.4	4.3	2.3	1.4	0.1
Operating profits after losses	0.7	–0.2	–4.3	–1.3	0.6	1.2
Memorandum item:						
Capital adequacy ratios						
According to pre-1991 rules	6.8	7.8	10.8	9.0	12.0	–
BIS standards, 1991 onwards	–	–	7.1	8.6	10.5	12.4
Savings banks [4]						
Net interest revenues	4.4	3.9	3.8	4.3	4.7	4.2
Other operating revenues	0.5	0.7	0.6	0.8	1.5	0.5
Operating costs	3.4	3.2	3.5	3.2	3	2.9 [5]
Operating profits before losses	1.5	1.4	0.9	1.9	3.2	1.7
Loan losses [3]	0.5	1.3	2.1	1.8	1.2	0.4
Operating profits after losses	1.0	0.1	–1.2	0	2	1.3
Memorandum item:						
Capital adequacy ratios						
According to pre-1991 standards	7.0	5.7	7	8	10.8	–
BIS rules from 1991 onwards	–	–	8.3	11.2	14.4	14.9

1. Parent banks.
2. Including write-downs and losses on sales of fixed assets.
3. Includes losses resulting from bank guarantees.
4. 24 largest banks for the period 1991-92; 30 largest banks for the period 1993-94.
5. Affected by one-off additional set-aside for pension expenditure.
Source: Bank of Norway, *Stortingsmelding nr. 39* "Bankkrisen og utviklingen i den norske banknaeringen 1994" and *Bank profitability*, 1981-1990, OECD, Paris, 1992.

increased competition among providers of time deposits, as an expanded supply of short-term (government) securities in recent years has offered attractive alternatives to investors. Spreads on short-term loans display less of a downward trend, except for the period 1989 to 1991, as lending rates responded with a lag to the sharp decline in funding rates after the floating of the currency.

The substantial improvement of banks' balance sheets over 1993 and 1994 suggests that bank lending has been largely freed from supply constraints. Indeed, after declines in the early 1990s, bank credit has recovered in the last

Figure 12. **CREDIT SUPPLY INDICATORS**

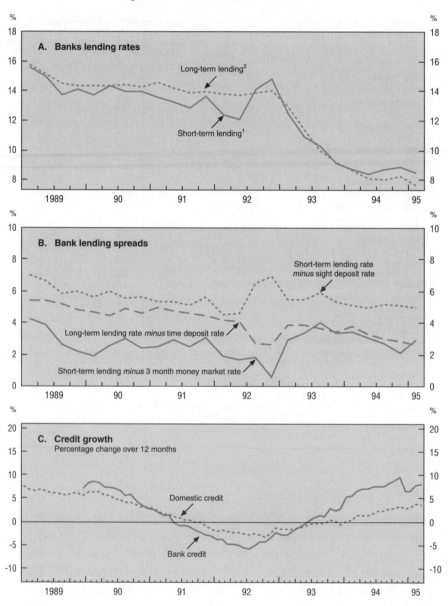

1. One year or less.
2. Over one year.
Source: Bank of Norway; OECD, *Main Economic Indicators.*

Table 7. **Sources of domestic credit expansion**

Percentage change from previous year

	Level End 1990 Nkr billion	1991	1992	1993	1994
Commercial and savings banks[1]	395.0	−2.2	−1.5[3]	3.3	6.9
State banks[2]	158.7	8.2	6.5	−2.4	−1.8
Mortgage institutions	128.7	−19.1	−20.3[3]	−17.8	−4.5
Life insurance institutions	65.5	13.6	8.8[3]	−7.7	−7.4
Bond and certificate market[4]	60.4	5.2	−2.7	14.3	4.3
Other	41.4	−12.9	−12.1	−11.1	15.3
Total domestic credit	849.7	−1.6	−1.4	−0.5	3.0

1. Including the Postal Savings Bank.
2. Excluding loan of the Municipal Bank.
3. Growth rates for 1992, are adjusted for the conversion of Bolig og Naeringskredit A/S from a mortgage institution to a bank in autumn 1992.
4. Adjusted for non-residents' holdings of private and municipal bonds issued in Norway.
Source: Bank of Norway.

two years, spurred by increased consumer confidence, lower interest rates and an associated revival of credit demand for residential investment (Figure 12, Panel C). With bank credit accounting for almost half of the total domestic credit stock, overall credit growth expanded in late 1994, by around 3 per cent over a year earlier (Table 7).[7] Reversing a trend observed previously, loans by the State banks fell relative to other sources of credit expansion in 1993 and, more significantly, in 1994, as favourable lending-rate differentials *vis-à-vis* commercial and savings banks were largely undone (Table 7, see also Chapter III). Such differentials occurred because the lending rates of commercial and savings banks were immediately adjusted after the fall in market rates in 1993, while those of State banks responded with some lag.

Monetary aggregates

Growth in narrow money supply (M1) was sustained in 1993 and 1994, reflecting the revival of economic activity but also a narrowing of the differential between interest rates on sight and time deposits, which reduced the opportunity cost of holding near money (Figure 13). The latter factor contributed to depress the growth rate of the broad money aggregate M2 (M1 + time deposits) relative to M1 in 1993, but in 1994 M1 and M2 growth numbers converged again as the

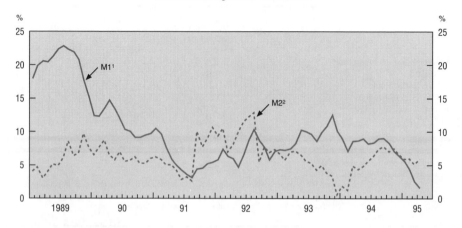

Figure 13. **MONETARY AGGREGATES**
Per cent change over 12 months

1. Cash, demand deposits and unused credit held by the public; each observation represents a 3-month right-adjusted moving average.
2. M1 plus time deposits.
Source: OECD, *Main Economic Indicators.*

differential between sight and time deposits stabilised. Two technical factors have also affected growth rates in M2 in recent years, notably the abolition, in August 1991, of tax-favoured savings deposits not included in the broad money aggregate (boosting M2 year-on-year growth rates in the subsequent twelve months) and a fall in accrued interest earnings entailed by the drop in interest rates (which led to a virtual halt in broad money expansion by the end of 1993).[8]

The fiscal stance

Towards a tighter orientation in 1993 and 1994

According to official estimates, the fiscal policy stance moved towards restriction in 1993 following several years of easing, with the cyclically-adjusted State deficit (net of debt interest payments and oil revenues) rising by ¼ per cent of mainland GDP after increasing by around 2 percentage points in each of the four preceding years (Figure 14). The 1993 budget outcome combined a signifi-

Figure 14. **STATE BUDGET BALANCE**
As a percentage of mainland GDP

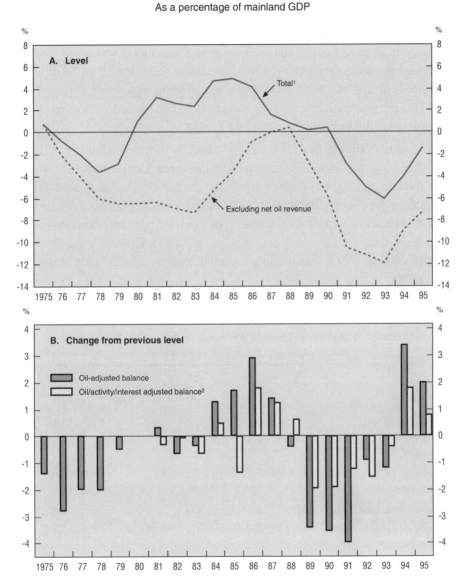

Note: Data for 1993 and 1994 are estimates; for 1995, projections.
1. As a percentage of total GDP.
2. Adjusted for cyclical developments, petroleum income, foreign interest payments, capital transactions and transfers from the Bank of Norway.
Source: Norwegian Ministry of Finance.

cant deceleration in expenditure growth with a higher contribution from the government's oil activities, limiting the increase in the central government deficit to 0.2 per cent of GDP from 2.6 per cent in 1992 (Table 8). As local government finances remained in broad balance, such near stabilisation was also reflected in the general government position, where the deficit fell from 2.3 of GDP in 1992 to 2.1 per cent in 1993. Such an outcome was slightly better than expected in the initial Budget proposal, due to unexpected oil windfalls and somewhat stronger economic growth than initially projected (Table 9).

The draft National Budget for 1994, which was presented to the Parliament in October 1993, announced enhanced efforts towards fiscal consolidation, entailing a moderate budgetary tightening – by $1/2$ per cent of mainland GDP as measured by the change in the Ministry of Finance's structural budget balance. In conjunction with an expected economic growth of 1.7 per cent, the non-oil deficit was projected to fall to 11.7 per cent of mainland GDP from an estimated 12.8 per cent in 1993. Expenditure restraint, mainly focusing on transfers to

Table 8. **Government expenditure, revenue and net lending position**[1]

Percentage changes from previous year

	1991	1992	1993	1994[2]	1995[2]
Total expenditure[3]					
General government	7.2	6.1	3.8	2.6	1.6
Central government	7.1	6.5	3.6	2.5	1.0
Local government	5.0	4.0	1.8	2.7	3.8
Total revenue					
General government	2.0	2.1	3.0	6.0	4.9
Central government	–0.5	–0.5	3.1	7.2	5.9
Local government	5.3	4.9	1.8	5.5	0.8
Net lending, level, percentage of GDP					
General government	0.3	–2.3	–2.1	–0.2	1.5
Central government	0.5	–2.6	–2.8	–0.8	1.3
Local government	–0.2	0.0	0.0	0.5	–0.1
Memorandum item:					
Nominal GDP	3.9	2.4	4.5	5.4	7.6

1. According to National Accounts definitions, except for central and local governments which are on an administrative basis.
2. Estimates and official projections contained in the 1995 Revised National Budget (May 1995).
3. Excluding capital injections in public enterprises.
Source: Norwegian Ministry of Finance, the 1995 National Budget (October and December versions) and 1995 Revised National Budget (May 1995).

Table 9. **State budget balance: projections and outcomes**

Percentage of GDP[1]

	1993		1994		1995	
	Budget	Outcome	Budget	Outcome[2]	Budget	Revised budget[2]
Budget balance before loan transactions	−6.8	−6.0	−6.1	−3.7	−2.6	−0.7
Net contribution from oil activities	3.6	3.8	3.5	3.3	3.9	4.6
Oil-adjusted budget balance[3]	−12.5	−11.9	−11.7	−8.5	−7.9	−6.5
Revenues[4]	45.7	45.8	45.8	46.7	45.5	45.5
Expenditures[5]	58.2	57.6	57.5	55.1	53.4	52.1
Change in structural budget balance[6]	−0.3	−0.4	0.5	1.8	0.8	0.8
Memorandum items:						
Local government balance	0.1	0.0	0.0	0.5	−0.2	−0.1
Mainland GDP volume growth	1.8	2.0	1.7	3.9	2.4	3.1

1. Mainland GDP in the case of oil-adjusted and structural balances.
2. Ministry of Finance estimates, May 1995.
3. Before loan transactions, adjusted for government net oil revenues.
4. Excluding oil revenues.
5. Excluding oil expenditure.
6. Adjusted for cyclical developments, petroleum income, foreign interest payments, capital transactions and transfers from Bank of Norway.
Source: Norwegian Ministry of Finance, National Budgets.

households, was to bear the brunt of this move. At the same time, the net contribution from oil proceeds was expected to remain broadly unchanged from a year before, implying a fall in the State deficit from 7.1 per cent of GDP in 1993 (October estimate, subsequently revised down to 6 per cent) to a projected 6.1 per cent in 1994.

Due essentially to the unexpected strength of the mainland economy, the State's 1994 non-oil deficit turned out to be much lower than initially projected – at 8.5 per cent of mainland GDP (May 1995 estimate). To some extent, this development also reflects the fact that government revenues were boosted by the rise in excise taxes in the summer subsequent to the Revised National Budget presented in May 1994.[9] With net oil revenues right on target, the overall State deficit fell from 6.0 per cent of GDP in 1993 to 3.7 per cent in 1994, while the central government's net borrowing position improved by about the same amount, from 2.8 per cent of GDP to 0.8 per cent.[10] As the recovery also triggered a surge in *local* government revenues, the general government net borrowing fell from 2.1 per cent of GDP in 1993 to 0.2 per cent in 1994.

31

Further tightening in 1995

With the recovery firmly entrenched, the government took additional restrictive measures in the National Budget proposal for 1995, which was presented to the Parliament in October 1994. Corrected for outlays related to unemployment, investment on the Norwegian Continental Shelf and technical one-off factors, growth in nominal State expenditure was restrained to 2 per cent, which broadly corresponds to a zero change in volume terms.[11] Major cuts in subsidies – of the order of $^2/_3$ per cent of mainland GDP – formed the centrepiece of this package, together with a growth limitation of public investment and consumption (to 0.3 per cent in real terms). On the revenue side, tax increases of roughly NKr 2 billion were announced, in part reflecting measures adopted in the Revised 1994 Budget. The resulting tighter fiscal stance – evidenced by a rise in the official structural budget indicator by $^3/_4$ per cent of mainland GDP – was projected to reduce the State's non-oil deficit from 9.1 per cent of mainland GDP in 1994 (October 1994 estimate) to 7.9 per cent in 1995 (Table 9). Consequently, with net oil income rising somewhat, the overall State deficit was set to drop from an estimated 4.6 per cent of GDP in 1994 to 2.6 per cent in 1995.

As foreseen in the budget proposal for 1995, further consolidation measures were announced in the December 1994 Budget Bill to counter possible adverse confidence effects on financial markets of the No-vote in the EU referendum. They included, in particular, a rise in the VAT rate by 1 percentage point to 23 per cent, which increased the projected tax take in 1995 by NKr 4 billion or $^2/_3$ per cent of mainland GDP. In conjunction with an upward revision of other revenues (including oil proceeds), the 1995 Bill projected a non-oil and overall deficit for the State budget of 7.0 and 1.4 per cent of mainland and total GDP respectively – the lowest levels since 1990. To prevent higher tax revenues resulting from stronger economic activity from spilling over into increased local spending, the initial December budget raised the State's share in the income tax take,[12] thus leaving total local revenues roughly unchanged in nominal terms from their 1994 level. As a result, local governments' net financial position was estimated to drop from a surplus of 0.5 per cent of GDP in 1994 to a deficit of 0.2 per cent in 1995. The substantial projected improvement in the general government position from a deficit of 0.9 per cent in 1994 (December estimate) to a surplus of 0.8 per cent in 1995 was thus accounted for by a reduction in the central government deficit.

The Revised National Budget for 1995 released in May reiterates the tight fiscal orientation implied by the December 1994 Bill, with the State's structural budget balance projected to improve by ¾ per cent of GDP (Table 9). Unadjusted for the impact of the business cycle, the non-oil State deficit is expected to attain 6½ per cent of mainland GDP, down by roughly 1½ per cent from the estimate in the December 1994 Budget Bill. Similarly, the projected overall surplus (including oil proceeds) of the general government has been revised upwards to 1½ per cent of total GDP.

Medium-term budget prospects

In the two Budget proposals and the Revised Budget for 1995, the government reiterated its commitment to fiscal consolidation in the medium term as stipulated earlier in the Long-Term Programme 1994-1997. This commitment was meant to keep public expenditure growth below the rate of growth of mainland GDP, which, with tax revenues broadly remaining constant as a share of mainland GDP, implies a progressive reduction of the oil-adjusted deficit. In so doing, three objectives are to be pursued: *i)* to build up the necessary financial assets to finance counter-cyclical policies in future downturns; *ii)* to contain inflation expectations and keep interest rates low; and *iii)* to relieve long-term strains on public finance from the expected decline in oil revenues and increase in welfare spending due to the ageing of the population (see Chapter IV).

An official update of the medium-term budget outlook contained in the 1995 National Budget projected a stabilisation of the non-oil general government deficit at around 5 per cent of GDP by 1998 (Figure 15, Panel A). This projection assumed a cut in the ratio of primary expenditure (*i.e.* excluding debt interest payments) to mainland GDP to around 60 per cent (from 62 per cent in 1994), and the maintenance of the tax ratio (excluding oil related revenues) at 52-53 per cent. While contributing to make the public finance position sustainable in the long run, such an evolution would also consolidate the sharp increase in the tax ratio that occurred in the period 1983-88. As can be inferred from Figure 15, Panel B, this increase was indeed largely of a structural, non-cyclical nature. The projections also suggest that the rise in government spending that took place during the period of fiscal easing from 1988 to 1992 will not be reversed in the future (Figure 15, Panel C). As a result, the room for reducing the relatively high tax burden will be limited, which, as argued in the next chapter, may impinge upon the functioning of the labour market and adversely affect the flexibility of the mainland economy.

Figure 15. **MEDIUM TERM TRENDS IN GENERAL GOVERNMENT FINANCE**

As a percentage of mainland GDP

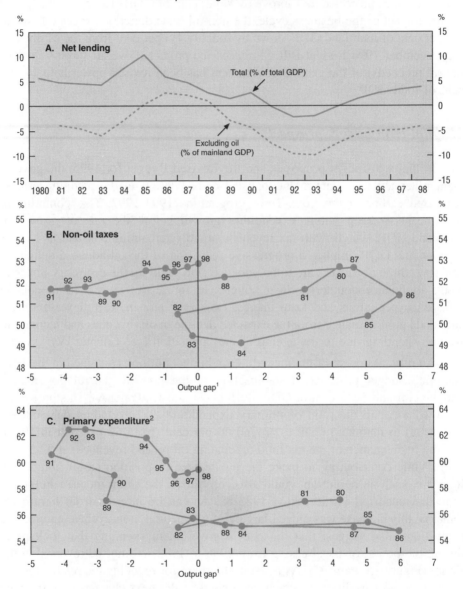

1. The gap between actual and trend mainland GDP as a percentage of trend mainland GDP.
2. Expenditure excluding interest on public debt.
Source: 1995 National Budget, OECD, *Quarterly National Accounts,* and OECD Secretariat.

III. Progress in structural reform

The structural measures adopted since 1993 have largely aimed at consolidating and extending the large-scale reform programme initiated in the early 1990s. The main focus of this programme has been to increase efficiency in the provision of goods and services by exposing Norwegian producers to more external competition in order to improve long-term growth performance. This appears all the more necessary given that the Norwegian economy is subject to volatility in income from oil and gas production. Indeed, uncertainties attached to future proceeds from the petroleum sector (see Chapter IV) would require more flexible product and labour markets to facilitate adjustments to unexpected swings in offshore revenues.

This basic orientation has not been modified as a result of the No-vote in the EU referendum in November 1994. Indeed, the government has reiterated its commitments to structural reform implied by the EEA-agreement which became effective 1 January 1994. The paragraphs below review the structural initiatives taken over the last two years and identify the scope for further action. The areas covered are the labour market, taxation, competition policy, government subsidies, public sector management, financial services and environment.

The labour market

Labour market reform continues to be a main concern in Norway as, at 7½ per cent of the labour force in early 1995 – including persons enrolled in Active Labour Market Programmes (ALMP) – the rate of unemployment is still relatively high by past Norwegian standards. The strong growth in employment recorded since the second half of 1993 prompted the authorities to reduce the number of participants in ALMP from 58 000 in 1994 to 45 000 by the second half of 1995, while also improving the *effectiveness* of these programmes through a better targeting on young and long-term unemployed and on specific segments in the labour market where bottlenecks are likely to emerge with the current recovery. Moreover, subject to collaboration with equivalent public institutions, private job-intermediation agencies are now permitted, with a view to improving the matching of supply and demand. In January 1995, the government proposed a reform of the unemployment insurance system, including a limitation of the total duration of benefits, from virtually indefinite at present to three years (156 weeks) as of 1996.[13] The level of benefits would remain unchanged over this three-year spell, compared to the present system where benefits are reduced after 80 weeks of unemployment.

While the above initiatives should, on balance, be judged positively, new legislation on job security implemented in the last two years does not invariably go in the direction of improving the functioning of the labour market. Although favourable effects may be expected from the extension of legal trial periods for young and inexperienced job-seekers (who in recent years registered above-average unemployment rates), the recent further limitation to the use of fixed-term employment contracts – whose previous regulation was already seen as the most restrictive in the OECD area[14] – may have an adverse impact on employment. Indeed, experience in other OECD countries suggests that perspectives for unemployed people to obtain durable employment typically improve after they have accepted a temporary or fixed-term contract.[15] The prohibition on dismissing staff whose tasks are to be contracted out, also entailed by the new legislation, seems inconsistent with policies encouraging sub-contracting by local governments (see below).

There is still considerable scope for reform of labour market policies. As argued in last year's *Economic Survey* and in the *OECD Jobs Study*, the high level of unemployment compensation in Norway has created a "wage floor" below which incentives for accepting a job rather than relying on a benefit are very weak. As a result, work disincentives for unemployed low-income workers are very high as their net gain on income when accepting a job amounts to only 20 to 30 per cent (taking into account both the loss in benefit and the impact of tax progression). Moreover, as argued by the Norwegian Commission on Youth Unemployment, real wage costs for youngsters with little work experience and/or incomplete education tend to exceed their marginal productivity, limiting the employment opportunities for the people concerned. Hence the need for a policy focusing on reducing wage costs of low-skilled job seekers, with the possibility of meeting solidarity concerns arising from a wider wage distribution through the tax system (at present, as shown in Figure 16, Norway has the most compressed wage distribution in the OECD area). As indicated by the Norwegian Employment Commission (NEC),[16] wage developments should also take greater account of regional differences in labour market conditions.

Taxation

Adjustments in the tax system in the period under review have resulted in a further strengthening of tax progressivity. For example, the imputed rent income for owner-occupied dwellings with an assessed value exceeding NKr 440 000 was increased in 1995. In 1994 the top rate for wealth taxes was raised from 1.3 to 1.5 per cent for net wealth exceeding NKr 530 000 for singles and NKr 570 000 for married couples. In June 1995, the Parliament adopted a modification of the so-called "split-model" – a method used to divide assessed income of self-employed into capital and labour components, each taxed in different ways. In the previous system a ceiling of NKr 1.3 million applied to labour income, with earnings above that amount considered as capital income and, as such, taxed at a rate of 28 per cent, rather than around 50 per cent (which is the marginal tax rate of labour income at that level). This system thus favoured self-employed people, especially liberal professions, as earnings from labour used to exceed the threshold for assessed wage income. In order to remove this bias, the new system – which will be effective as of January 1996 – introduces different tax regimes for liberal professions and other self-employed people. These involve a rise in the existing threshold (from NKr 1.3 million to NKr 2.9 million) for liberal professions and the creation of two additional tax brackets for other categories of self employed.[17]

With the above changes, and the recent increases in indirect taxation (Chapter II), a fundamental feature of the Norwegian tax system – very high average rates – has become even more pronounced in the last two years. According to the 1995 National Budget, the share of non-petroleum taxes in mainland GDP will exceed 53 per cent, the highest level – on a comparable basis – across OECD countries.[18] This goes together with a marginal tax wedge (i.e. the difference between the cost of employing someone and the amount of after-tax con-

Figure 16. WAGE DISPERSION

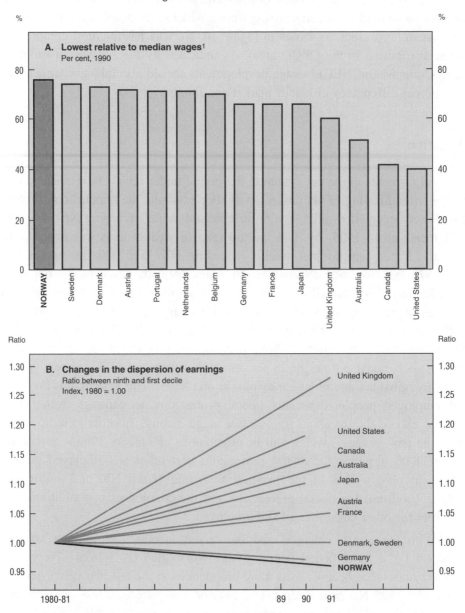

A. Lowest relative to median wages[1]
Per cent, 1990

(%)

NORWAY, Sweden, Denmark, Austria, Portugal, Netherlands, Belgium, Germany, France, Japan, United Kingdom, Australia, Canada, United States

B. Changes in the dispersion of earnings
Ratio between ninth and first decile
Index, 1980 = 1.00

Ratio

United Kingdom
United States
Canada
Australia
Japan
Austria
France
Denmark, Sweden
Germany
NORWAY

1980-81   89 90 91

1. "Low paid" means here earning a wage corresponding to the lowest decile on the wage distribution.
Source: Danish Economic Council, 1991, Copenhagen; OECD, *Employment Outlook,* 1993.

sumption an employee can finance out of his take-home pay) of about 60 per cent of the employees' compensation, which is comparable to the average for the European OECD countries and well above that for the rest of the OECD area (Figure 17). As argued in the *OECD Jobs Study*, such high levels of marginal taxation tend to adversely affect work motivation and lead to lower levels of employment.[19] In this regard, a recent Norwegian study[20] estimated the cost of a marginal public expenditure programme at 150 per cent of the initial spending outlay due to the production and income losses associated with the additional taxes required to finance such a programme.

Although the scope for reducing tax rates on labour by broadening the tax base is limited (Table 10), there is a specific area (*owner-occupied housing*) where this would nevertheless seem appropriate. Indeed, tax authorities typically assess house values at 20 to 30 per cent of the market price and calculate the imputed rent income at a rate much below the normal return on other types of investment (2.5 per cent of the assessed value for all but the most expensive houses).[21] This assessment method considerably reduces the tax base for owner-

Figure 17. **OVERALL MARGINAL TAX WEDGE**[1]

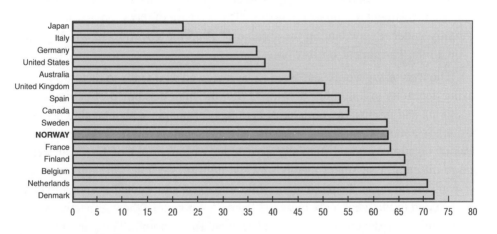

1. The overall marginal tax wedge includes income taxes, employers' and employees' public social security contributions and consumption taxes. It is defined for a person receiving earnings at the level of an average production worker.
Source: OECD, *Job Study,* 1994.

Table 10. **Tax structure**

1992

	Income and profit taxes	Social security and payroll taxes	Property taxes	Indirect taxes[1]	Total
	Per cent of GDP[2]				
Norway[3]	**15.2**	**14.4**	**1.7**	**19.1**	**50.4**
Other Nordic countries[4]	22.9	9.4	1.6	14.7	48.6
OECD Europe	14.0	11.6	1.7	13.4	40.6
OECD	14.3	10.2	2.0	12.2	38.8
	Per cent of total tax take				
Norway[3]	**30.2**	**28.6**	**3.4**	**37.9**	**100**
Other Nordic countries[4]	47.1	19.3	3.3	30.2	100
OECD Europe	34.0	28.1	4.3	33.5	100
OECD	37.0	25.9	5.5	31.6	100

1. Including "other taxes" which accounts for less than 2 per cent of GDP.
2. Excluding petroleum activities in the case of Norway.
3. Excluding tax proceeds from petroleum activities.
4. Excluding Iceland.
Source: 1995 National Budget and Revenue Statistics of OECD Member countries, 1965-1993, 1994.

occupiers, with respect to both income and wealth taxation, and represents an implicit subsidy discriminating against other instruments of wealth formation such as investment in financial assets. The system of taxation of housing is currently under review, and in the autumn of 1995 the government will submit a report to the Parliament on this issue.

The *wealth tax* would also need to be reviewed as it tends to distort personal saving decisions in a number of ways. *First*, the high combined effective rate of wealth tax and income tax on interest earnings for people with a taxable net asset position – about 50 per cent – discourages personal savings. *Second*, effective rates of taxation vary substantially across the various types of financial wealth due to different assessment methods (while uniform tax rates are applied except for pension savings). In particular, while unquoted and quoted corporate shares are included in the wealth tax base at 30 and 75 per cent of their respective value, bonds and bank deposits are assessed at their full amount. This has *inter alia* induced the development of tax evasion schemes, among which the creation of non-quoted firms whose only purpose is to cover up personal holdings of quoted shares and bonds. In view of these drawbacks, the government is considering some change in the tax assessment of wealth in order to make it more neutral. *Third*, financial wealth built up through occupational pension schemes being fully exempt from wealth tax, such savings are favourably treated relative to other forms of capital accumulation. This is particularly problematic as pension funds are faced with a legal constraint on the amount of money they can invest in securities (see below). Hence, the favourable tax treatment of private pensions – which is currently being reconsidered by the government[22] – indirectly acts against investment in bonds and shares.

Finally, given that Norway shares a long border with Sweden, one of the new members of the European Union, there is a case for harmonising Norwegian *indirect taxes* with those in the EU. A recent study suggests that EU accession of Sweden is unlikely to have large immediate effects on cross-border trade, as indirect taxes there are still relatively high.[23] Nevertheless, with 40 per cent of the Norwegian population living in border regions, the sustainability of the present level of indirect taxation in Norway will become more dependent on developments in the EU.

Competition policy

The new competition law effective since January 1994, which replaces the Price Act of 1953, provides the Norwegian authorities with a clear mandate to supervise business practices and to act against anti-competitive activities if necessary. Direct price controls being completely abandoned from the legislation, the new law institutionalises the reorientation of policies towards effective competition on product markets. In particular, the authorities can act against public enterprises who financially support subsidiaries that are in competition with private suppliers. While they cannot impose administrative fines or other sanctions, the competition authorities are charged with examining whether there are cases for prosecution or caution, and pass on their deliberations to the competent authority (the police, the ministry supervising the activity of a specific public enterprise, etc.).

As part of its action to strengthen competition policy, the government has put forward a programme of deregulation of domestic markets dominated by state monopolies:[24]

- from 1 April 1994, both public and private domestic airlines have access to all domestic routes. This has led to a significant increase in capacity on the most important routes, without – so far – adverse effects on sparsely served destinations.[25] From 1997, foreign airlines will be given access to the domestic market as well. These measures complement the EEA-agreement which implied that *international* flights within the EEA-area should be opened to all airlines as of 1 July 1994;
- in conjunction with the implementation of the GATT-agreements, the import and distribution monopoly in the grain market – operated through the state-owned enterprise Statkorn – will be abolished in 1995;
- the role of regional monopolies on hydropower has been further reduced, complementing the successful reform of the electricity market in 1991 (see Box 1);
- to help contain public health expenditure, parallel imports of drugs have been allowed and the state's wholesale monopoly in the drugs distribution has been abolished. Moreover, retail prices of prescribed drugs are henceforth determined by actual costs of purchase and distribution rather than through a fixed mark-up on wholesale prices, reducing the incentive for pharmacies to sell expensive brands.

To prepare the ground for further deregulation in the future, the administrative structure of several state monopoly enterprises has been changed. On 1 November 1994, the public telecommunication enterprise was transformed into a state-owned stock company *Telenor*, providing its management with more discretion in framing and implementing new business strategies. The new company, though providing various services in competition with private suppliers, will maintain its monopoly on network management. Administrative reforms are also being implemented in the road transportation agency, entailing a split between its regulatory and production activities.

The reforms put in place thus far tend to be mutually supportive. Those concerning the administration of public enterprises are most effective when the market behaviour of these enterprises is checked by the potential entry of new competitors and a strong competition authority. The latter should ensure, in particular, that government appropriations and monopoly profits are not used to subsidise activities on markets where free competition prevails. It is important in this regard that the administrative control of firms be facilitated by transparent

Box 1. **Reforms in the electricity market**

Prior to the Energy Act of 1991, the regional supply of electricity was dominated by local monopolies, resulting from combined ownership of hydro power plants and a local grid system. This gave rise to monopoly rents and excess capacity in power generation, also encouraged by municipalities who used local electricity supply as a vehicle for revenue raising. The new law opened up the electricity grid to all producers and consumers in the country, thus breaking up local monopolies. It also required electricity companies to keep separate accounts for power generation and the sale of grid services, in order to avoid cross-subsidisation of the former activity by the latter. The reform has radically changed the electricity market in Norway, which now allows customers to shop around for the best (long-term) contracts, while also offering a possibility of buying substantial amounts of electricity in the spot market.

As a favourable side effect, the reform has led to increased international trade in electricity with Sweden, Denmark and Germany, exploiting the differences in cost structure between conventional (coal-burning) power plants in these countries and Norwegian hydro power. Conventional plants typically have surplus capacity during the night, which is potentially available at low marginal costs, while these tend to be very high during the day. Hydro-power plants, by contrast, are able to tap energy at any time of the day from their huge storage reservoirs. As a result, the marginal costs of hydro power plants tend to exceed those of coal-burned power stations during the night, while the reverse is the case during the day. It is hence profitable for hydro power plants to import electricity from coal-burning plants at night, while the latter benefit from buying hydro power during daily peak hours.

The 1995 National Budget introduced a number of new measures to further enhance competition in the electricity sector. First, with effect from 1 January 1995, cost barriers of switching from one supplier to another have been reduced through a ban on forced installation of new metering equipment – which proved particularly constraining for small users of electricity. In addition, an experiment is being carried out with a secondary market for electricity-delivery contracts. The authorities have also shown strong interest for further developing a Nordic common market for electricity, but so far this has to await developments in the other Scandinavian countries where the reform process is less advanced.

accounts, which is best achieved by splitting up public enterprises into their constituent parts. For Telenor, for example, that would imply a split into a company for network management (representing a natural monopoly) and one for other services.[26] Similarly, municipalities could be encouraged to divide their hydropower activities into separate companies for electricity production and grid management.[27] Over time, that would also facilitate a concentration of grid management into a smaller number of operators to reap economies of scale.

Government subsidies

Total government support to various economic sectors has remained broadly unchanged at nearly 4 per cent of GDP since the early 1990s – which is well above the OECD average (Table 11). This masks, however, a significant reduction in direct subsidies in recent years, especially to agriculture (including fisheries) and state enterprises. By contrast, tax expenditures have been boosted through exemptions for electricity tax, affecting energy intensive industries in particular. In the 1995 National Budget, the government has announced a reduction in industrial support, recognising its distortionary effects. The largest cuts are envisaged in shipbuilding, as a consequence of the OECD agreement in this area, which prohibits all production-based subsidies for building and repairing ships as from 1994. Moreover, some modest further reduction in agricultural subsidies is envisaged, consistent with the new GATT agreement.

Table 11. **Government subsidies**

NKr billion, 1994 prices

	1990	1991	1992	1993	1994
Direct subsidies	23.1	23.0	22.8	22.1	22.0
of which:					
Agriculture, forestry and fishing	15.4	15.5	14.5	13.5	13.2
Shipbuilding	1.0	1.4	1.8	2.0	1.4
State-owned firms	1.4	0.4	0.4	0.3	0.4
Other manufacturing	3.5	3.6	3.9	3.5	4.0
Private services[1]	0.6	0.7	0.9	0.8	1.0
Other[2]	1.2	1.6	1.5	2.0	2.0
Tax expenditure[3]	0.4	1.0	1.2	2.8	3.3
of which:					
Exemption for electricity tax[4]	0	0.2	0.4	2.0	2.5
Exemption for mineral oil tax[5]	0.4	0.8	0.9	0.8	0.8
Total subsidies	23.5	24.0	24.0	24.9	25.3
As a per cent of mainland GDP	3.8	3.8	3.8	3.8	3.8

1. Excludes costs associated with banking rescue operations.
2. Includes the State's subsidies to firms in the context of active labour market programmes.
3. Excluding exemption from CO_2 tax in specific industries.
4. Mainly manufacturing.
5. Mainly sea transportation.
Source: 1995 National Budget and Statistics Norway.

As argued in last year's Survey, the scope for cuts in agricultural support is still substantial, even when taking into account the goals of self-sufficiency in food supply and the preservation of rural population in remote areas. Agriculture currently receives more than half of total government support and also benefits from a high degree of protection against imports from abroad (Table 11). Gauged by the Producer Subsidy Equivalent (PSE), agricultural support amounts to almost 80 per cent of the production value – or almost twice the OECD and EU averages (Figure 18). Complying with the GATT agreement – which implies an estimated reduction in support from the present NKr 19 billion (or US$30 000 per full-time employed) to NKr 16½ billion by 2000[28] – will mark a significant departure from the present structure, but further progress in this direction is warranted. Apart from shipbuilding, budgetary support to the manufacturing sector also remains high by international standards.

Figure 18. **AGRICULTURAL SUPPORT**
Producer Subsidy Equivalents, 1993[1]

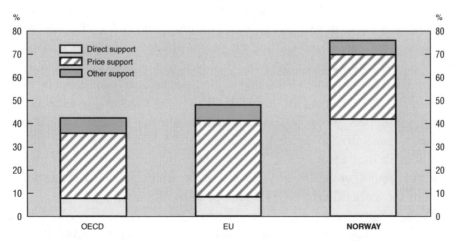

1. As per cent of production value.
Source: OECD.

Public sector management

Policies in this area have essentially focused on the activities of local government, notably in the fields of education, social services and health care. The main objective has been to simplify the detailed standards set by the State and encourage the use of broad performance criteria, leaving municipalities and counties with larger freedom to decide how to carry out their tasks. At the same time, cuts in state transfers and the increasing use of public tendering are designed to induce municipalities to become more cost-conscious. Subcontracting has also been encouraged by making laundry, cleaning and construction services by local government departments subject to indirect taxation. Hence, a municipality can no longer save VAT by producing a service itself rather than using a private sector firm.

Although the overall performance of the *health sector* is considered satisfactory, both in terms of quality of the services provided and the overall costs,[29] in a recent White Paper[30] the government outlined some desirable reforms in this area. These focus on the hospital sector, where rapid technological developments have induced local administrations to build up new capacity in narrow disciplines, even in the smallest establishments. Modern equipment in hospitals is often underutilised and staff is not always sufficiently experienced.[31] Efforts to concentrate specialised disciplines in a smaller number of hospitals meet resistance from local authorities, particularly in remote or rural areas where staff reductions have a significant adverse impact on the local economy. To resolve this problem, the government has considered shifting the responsibility for hospital management from the local authorities to the State. However, as this approach turned out not to be feasible, the government decided to increase the State's influence by raising its share in the financing of hospitals. The state transfers will be used to encourage hospitals to concentrate specialised treatments in larger establishments and, more generally, to promote a division of labour between the different institutions in the health sector. To develop cost-consciousness, techniques for measuring output of health services are to be improved, thus enhancing the ability of the authorities to target resources more efficiently.

While conducive to a more productive public sector, the recently implemented or envisaged reforms in public administration leave the responsibility for delivering services mainly with local governments. Improving the allocation of public resources and enhancing cost-effectiveness may thus require tighter budget constraints at the local level. Future developments in this respect also depend upon the willingness of municipalities and counties to co-operate, with a view both to maximising scale economies and to preventing excess capacity.

Financial services

With the banking crisis of the early 1990s practically over (see Chapter II), recent government policies have aimed at completing regulatory reforms concerning safety nets in the financial industry. In a White Paper presented in April 1994, two areas for reform were identified. First, the present unlimited deposit insurance scheme was recognised as inducing bank managers to take excessive risks, as it allows systematic bail-out in case of insolvency. Second, there is a perception that the system for banking governance, *i.e.* the structure of ruling bodies, is lacking in transparency and clear attribution of responsibilities, and may thus have contributed to the banking crisis.[32]

In addition, a number of initiatives have been taken by the government with a view to bolstering the efficiency of the financial industry through enhanced competition and rationalisation. These are reflected in reduced staff and branch numbers (Figure 19, Panel A). While job cuts have on average been smaller than in other Nordic countries, *e.g.* Finland, the initial degree of overstaffing may also have been less marked (Figure 19, Panel B). As recommended in previous *OECD Surveys*,[33] there is also increased recognition of the need to reduce progressively the State's share in capital of the major commercial banks, which in the course of the banking crisis had become fully or partly State-owned (Table 12). The present policy – the result of a compromise between the various parties in the Parliament – allows for a full privatisation of Fokus Bank within the period 1995-96, while the State will keep a share of at least 50 per cent in Kreditkassen and Den norske Bank until the end of the current parliamentary period in 1997.

The role of the traditional State banks, such as the Housing Bank and the Industrial and Regional Development Fund (SND) is also being reviewed. In recent years, when growth was relatively weak, those banks were particularly active on the loan markets as they could extend lending at cheap interest rates. As a result, their share in the stock of credit increased from 19 per cent in 1990 to 22 per cent in 1993 (Figure 20, Panel A). This trend was reversed, however, with the 1995 National Budget which announced a cut of 11 per cent in total state

Figure 19. **RATIONALISATION IN THE BANKING SECTOR**

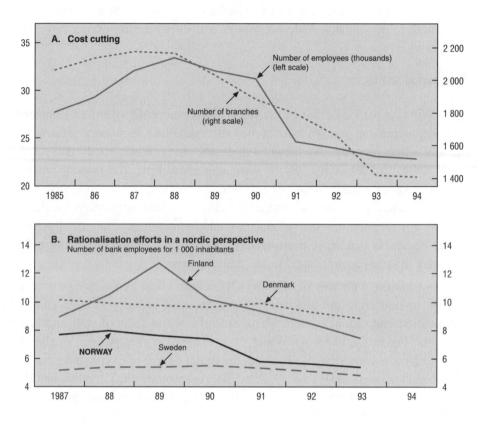

Source: Statistics Norway; Bank of Norway.

bank lending ceilings. In a period of expected strong credit growth, this should lead to a marked decline in the market share of the State banks. Moreover, in March 1995 the official Commission on State Banks recommended relatively far-reaching reforms such as *i)* curtailing the activities of the Housing Bank whose lending should be concentrated on clearly defined social objectives instead of being provided irrespective of the income and wealth position of the borrower; *ii)* providing transfers in the form of means-tested income support rather than subsidised loans; and *iii)* streamlining the volume of cheap loans to the business sector by merging the banks for agriculture and fisheries with SND.

Table 12. **Progress in bank privatisation**

State share of capital end of year, per cent

	Den norske Bank (DnB)	Kredit kassen Bank (CBK)	Fokus Bank (F.B)
1990	0	0	0
1991	0	100	100
1992	56	99	100
1993	69	69	98
1994	72	69	98
1997	Minimum 50	Minimum 50	– [1]
After 1997	Minimum 33	Minimum 33	– [1]

1. Government stake to be sold when judged to be commercially attractive.
Source: Ministry of Finance, *Stortingsmelding nr. 39* on Banking.

Figure 20. **IMPORTANCE OF THE STATE BANKS**

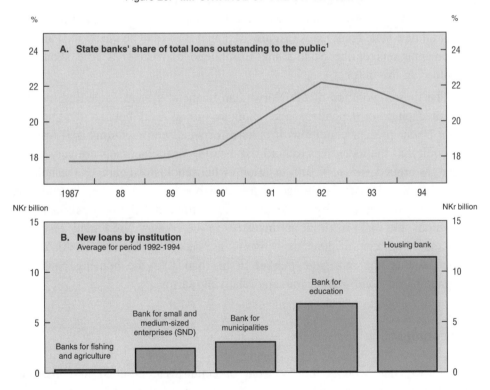

1. End of year figures.
Source: Ministry of Finance.

49

The increased international competition facing the Norwegian banking industry,[34] resulting from the implementation of the EEA agreement, creates pressure for a further reduction of state involvement. The rationale for continued state ownership of the two major existing commercial banks appears somewhat ambiguous in this regard. On the one hand, the stated policy is that these banks should function completely as commercial financial institutions, with profitability of activities as the overriding objective. On the other hand, the authorities consider it essential that control of these banks remain in "national hands" – *de facto* implying public ownership – apparently fearing that foreign owners might act against "Norwegian interests". Such a combination of potentially conflicting objectives could make state ownership of banks problematic, as it may induce the State to interfere in the credit policy of banks.[35] It would thus seem desirable for the long run efficiency of the Norwegian banking sector that ownership, over time, be completely returned to the private sector. As regards the state banks, the large-scale activities of the Housing Bank – accounting for nearly half of all new state bank loans (Figure 20, Panel B) – may be questioned and the recommendations of the State Bank Committee to reduce its role should be welcomed in this respect.

The future evolution of the Norwegian financial system, including markets for risk capital, is dependent upon policies going well beyond deregulation *per se*. Under present conditions it is hard for small and medium-sized firms to raise equity, as the incentives to hold risk-bearing financial assets are very weak. Indeed, as argued above, wealth taxation of households discourages the holding of such financial assets – quoted shares and bonds in particular. In addition, investments in securities by the social security fund and the occupational pensions funds, the main institutional investors in the country, are legally restricted to 15 and 20 per cent of their respective total assets (see Chapter IV). Also, with 70 per cent of the mortgage market in the hands of the housing bank, the mortgage-based bond market remains relatively narrow.

Environment

Norway has been at the forefront of countries committed to a rigorous environmental policy, and has actively supported international agreements aiming at reducing emissions of environmentally damaging substances with a regional or

Figure 21. **AIR POLLUTION INDICATORS**

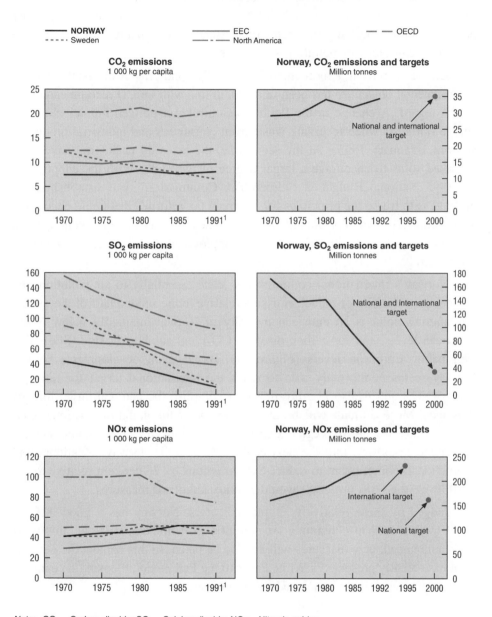

Note: CO_2 = Carbon dioxide; SO_2 = Sulphur dioxide; NOx = Nitrogin oxides.
1.   1992 for Norway, closest year for the other countries.
Source: Ministry of Finance; OECD, *Environmental data compendium, 1993.*

51

global impact. It also has taken measures to contain pollution with a primarily local impact. All these actions build to a large extent upon the ''the polluter pays'' principle, implying that firms or households are charged for the damage caused by emissions of polluting substances.

On the local front, a more intensive use of tax and price instruments to attain environmental objectives has been initiated, in line with OECD recommendations in this regard. A change in the Pollution Control Act obliged municipalities to charge full costs when receiving waste from consumers and industrial producers as from 1 January 1995. At the same time, the taxes on packaging have been reformed so as to encourage a larger degree of recycling. With the adoption of the 1995 National Budget, a ''Green Tax Commission'' was established. Its mandate is to frame the principles for ''a green tax reform'' that could encourage an economic growth considered as environmentally sustainable while, at the same time, consistent with a high level of employment and an overall unchanged tax burden.

Norway's international commitments relate essentially to air pollution, the aim being to stabilise or reduce emission relative to the second half of the 1980s. The starting point is an emission intensity in Norway markedly below North American levels, and for carbon dioxide (CO_2) and sulphur dioxide (SO_2), also well below European levels (Figure 21). Based upon developments so far, Norway seems comfortably able to reach the international target for nitrogen oxides (NO_x) and is also in a position to accomplish the national target for this substance. More difficult will be the attainment of the ambitious national CO_2 target; in fact, official Norwegian long-term projections of CO_2 emissions suggest further increases well into the next century.[36] As well, Norway's (national and international) commitment to reduce SO_2 emissions by 76 per cent relative to the 1980 level (the Oslo protocol) would require additional measures.

Judged by these relatively simple indicators, Norway has a good international track record in containing air pollution. Nonetheless, with the ambitious goals announced, new measures will need to be taken. In this context the government has recently presented a White Paper to the Parliament, focusing on enhancing cost-efficiency of emission-reduction policies.[37]

IV.   Petroleum wealth and public finance in the long run

The important stock of oil and gas in the North Sea represents the largest single source of wealth of the Norwegian economy. In managing this wealth, the Norwegian authorities have aimed to: *i)* maximise the (future) flow of revenues originating from the production of oil and gas; *ii)* channel a substantial part of these revenues through the budget to ensure that the whole society benefits from it; and *iii)* preserve an equitable share of the petroleum income for future generations through the build-up of public assets. While the first two objectives have largely been met, the last one is still a matter of concern, despite a comfortable net asset position of the government and fiscal surpluses likely to emerge in the years to come (see Chapter II).

Indeed, fiscal policy is faced with a major challenge in the long run, given the need to accommodate an expected fall in petroleum revenues after the present decade and a subsequent increase in welfare expenditure – public pensions in particular – due to the ageing of the population. Moreover, the public pension system is expected to become more costly, as a result of rising entitlements associated with the maturing of the system and the increased labour-market participation of women. Health care expenditure may also rise significantly, only partly offset by a fall in education spending. Although far from being a unique case in the OECD in these respects,[38] Norway stands out as a country where the share of public expenditure and taxation in GDP is already very high and the room for further increases correspondingly small. This raises the question as to how the public pension system should be managed and in what way current petroleum revenues could best be used to relieve long-run budgetary constraints.

These long-term issues form the main focus of this chapter. The first section briefly illustrates the importance of the petroleum sector as well as its interaction with the budget and the economy at large. This is followed by an assessment of the long-term outlook for oil and gas production and the related government proceeds. The chapter then discusses the overall development of the budget in the long run, with special emphasis on public pensions. The last section examines the policies currently followed in this regard and suggests further possible action.

Economic significance of the petroleum sector

The petroleum resources

The first discoveries of oil and gas in the Norwegian Continental Shelf (NCS) date back to the late 1960s. Petroleum production[39] actually started in 1971 on the *Ekofisk* field (discovered in 1969) in the extreme south-western part of Norway's North Sea territory, which is still one of the major production areas. Most other main fields currently in production or under development were discovered in the course of the 1970s and early 1980s, among which the *Statfjord* field (1971), the *Troll-West* field (1979) and the *Troll-East* field (1983). These fields are all located in the north-western part of Norway's North Sea territory, roughly level with the coasts of Bergen and Stavanger. In the mid-1970s an extensive network of pipelines was set up and has been gradually extended since, securing steady export flows of gas and oil from the North Sea to Great Britain and the European continent (Figure 22).

With a few exceptions, oil and gas resources in parts of the NCS which are located outside the North Sea, in particular the Norwegian Sea (along the Atlantic Coast) and the Barents Sea (close to the polar circle), have so far been relatively small and are more difficult to exploit due to difficult climatic conditions. According to recent estimates, about one-fifth and one-third of Norway's *discovered* and *total* remaining resources respectively – including those expected to be discovered given the geological structure of the NCS – are located in the Norwegian and Barents Seas (Table 13). The production licenses for the Norwegian Sea started being awarded in 1980 – with a first find in 1981 – and new acreage is being opened for exploration with the 15th licensing round in 1995. In the Barents Sea no petroleum has been produced to date.

As production of oil and gas has grown tremendously since the early 1970s (Figure 23), Norway has become a major global energy supplier. At present, the country is the seventh-biggest producer and the third-biggest net exporter of

Figure 22. **MAJOR PRODUCTION LOCATIONS AND PIPELINES IN THE NORTH SEA**

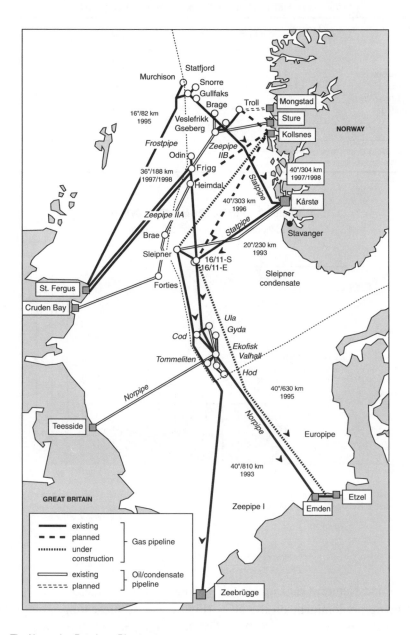

Source: The Norwegian Petroleum Directorate.

Table 13. **Norway's petroleum resources**

End 1994, billions of Standard cubic metres of Oil Equivalent

	North Sea	Norwegian Sea	Barents Sea	Total	of which: gaz (per cent)
Produced	1.63	0.00	0.00	1.63	26
Under development	2.61	0.22	0.00	2.83	47
Discoveries	1.40	0.55	0.30	2.25	67
Enhanced recovery [1]	0.5	0.00	0.00	0.50	0
Undiscovered	1.36	1.35	0.83	3.54	–
Total	7.50	2.12	1.13	10.75	–

1. Recoverable with improved technologies.
Source: Ministry of Finance.

Figure 23. **PETROLEUM EXTRACTION**

Millions of tonnes of oil equivalent

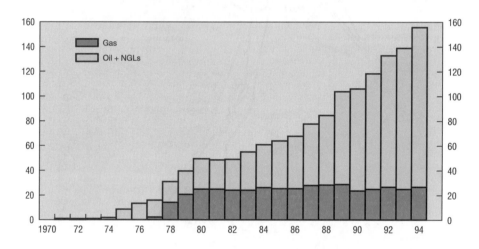

Source: Statistics Norway.

crude oil and Natural Gas Liquids (NGLs) in the world – these ''wet'' products so far being predominant on the NCS (Figure 24). Representing around 25 per cent of total extraction on the NCS to date, the production of ''dry'' natural gas is also sizeable, Norway being a major supplier of this product to the western part

Figure 24. **PRODUCTION AND NET EXPORTS OF CRUDE OIL**
1994, million barrels per day, including NGLs[1]

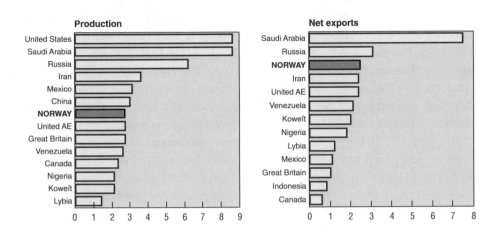

1. Natural gas liquids.
Source: MIE, Petroleum Economics Limited.

of Europe, and among the ten biggest net exporters in the world. As remaining resources contain more than 50 per cent dry gas (Table 13), its importance is bound to increase further in the future (see below). The significance of Norway as a producer of oil and gas contrasts sharply with the relatively modest size of the resources on the NCS in a global context. These resources, at current estimates, represent approximately only 1 per cent of total reserves in the world.

The government's involvement

The State is strongly engaged in the activities on the NCS and draws significant revenues from it. Its involvement entails: *i)* the *licensing* of acreage for development; *ii)* the presence on the NCS of a State-owned oil company (*Statoil*); *iii)* the State's own production facilities (the State's Direct Financial Interest) and *iv)* the special *tax regime* applying to oil companies active on the NCS.

Licensing policy

With some 30 (mostly foreign) oil companies engaged in operations on the NCS, the government has designed an extensive *licensing system* regulating their activities with respect to exploration, production and transportation of petroleum. The 1985 Petroleum Act, which contains the legal basis for the system, also stipulates that before every "licensing round" the area where drilling will take place must be authorised by the Parliament, the decision being conditional on a thorough assessment of the environmental, economic and social impact of the planned petroleum activities. The awarding of licenses is handled by the Ministry of Industry and Energy, and depends on an assessment of the experience and technological competence as well as the financial strength of the applying companies. The licenses are granted for a maximum of 40 years.[40] Even though the companies must apply individually, the Ministry usually grants a *joint* license to a group of companies designated to form a consortium. One company is appointed as the main operator within the consortium.

The government has used the licensing system extensively to steer the pace of extraction on the NCS. In the early stages of exploitation, the government's licensing policy aimed at moderating the rate of oil extraction with a view to maximising the wealth associated with the petroleum resources. This was seen as appropriate at a time when crude oil prices were expected to increase in the medium and long term, so that revaluation gains could be realised on the remaining petroleum reserves.[41] An extraction level of 90 million TOE (Tons of Oil Equivalent) per year was initially considered as a reasonable target in this regard. However, as large-scale investments on the NCS in the early 1980s turned out to be very profitable, the extraction level increased much more than initially envisaged, to above 130 million TOE in the early 1990s (Figure 23).

The State's oil company

On 2 June 1972 the State established an oil company *"Statoil"*, with the combined purpose of building up a national-based production infrastructure on the NCS and developing in-house technological know-how. This fully State-owned corporate enterprise has also become an important source of government revenues, with the same tax regime applied to it as to other oil companies on the NCS (see below) and the annual dividend pay-out amounting usually to 30 per cent of after tax operating profits.[42] Although managed as a normal corporate enterprise, the company has a special status resulting from two arrangements:

- until the fourteenth licensing round, which took place in 1993, Statoil was allocated a stake of at least 50 per cent in every joint production licence awarded (since 1985 this included the State Direct Financial Interest, see below). As a result, the company is by far the biggest producer on the NCS.[43] In the fourteenth round the allocation policy has been relaxed in this regard, with the State participation per license ranging from 40 to 65 per cent;
- Statoil heads two official bodies, the Gas Negotiation Committee and the Gas Supply Committee. The first Committee was established in 1986 to co-ordinate the negotiations of delivery contracts of natural gas on behalf of the industry. Two other Norwegian companies active in the energy sector – Norsk Hydro and Saga Petroleum – are also represented in this Committee. The Gas Supply Committee was set up in 1993 and regroups the twelve largest operators on the NCS. Its task is to advise the Ministry of Industry and Energy on the development of gas fields and the allocation of infrastructure and production capacity across gas delivery contracts.

Foreign companies usually welcome the presence of a large State enterprise on national territory as it ensures an adequate level of experience in the host country. Moreover, as the State provides neither financial support nor any guarantees on the company's borrowing, Statoil does not enjoy cost advantages which could lead to unfair competition. In fact, Statoil is free to develop its own strategy, as shown by its diversification into oil refinery activities after the oil-price drop in 1986. The company's room for manoeuvre has been further enhanced by a recent decision of the Parliament to lift constraints on Statoil participating in projects abroad.[44]

The State Direct Financial Interest

On 1 January 1985 the government created the *State Direct Financial Interest (SDFI)* which implied that a significant part of Statoil's profits henceforth accrued directly to the State and could not be retained by the company if it wished to do so. The purpose of this measure was to channel a greater part of the petroleum rent directly to the State as well as to reduce the company's ability to increase its capital base and become too independent from its formal owner. After this arrangement was implemented, all oil and gas extracted by Statoil had to be split into: *i)* a part owned by that company; and *ii)* a part owned by the State, with Statoil formally acting as an operator on the State's behalf. The allocation of petroleum resources between SDFI and Statoil, and the ensuing investment, extraction cost and profits, is determined by the government on an *ad hoc* basis when awarding the production licences.

Tax regime

When in the early 1970s the significance of the petroleum resources had become clear, the government stipulated that the profits from the operations on the NCS should "benefit the entire population" and should be used "to create a better society" through increased public spending on social security, culture, education, infrastructure and maintenance, as well as development of rural areas.[45] Lower taxes on mainland economic activities, a shorter working week and an increase in development aid were also considered as priority areas. In order to attain these goals, the government designed a system of taxation of petroleum profits which should ensure that the bulk of the benefits go to the government, without jeopardising the attractiveness of the NCS to foreign oil companies. According to the present oil tax regime endorsed in 1992, this system includes a standard 28 per cent corporate tax charged on profits net of depreciation allowance,[46] a special surtax of 50 per cent on these profits and a royalty of 8 to 16 per cent of gross sales on oil from fields cleared for development before 1 January 1986 (Table 14). Of less significance, in quantitative terms, are the acreage charge levied as a lump sum per square kilometre licensed, and the CO_2 charge created in the early 1990s. The royalty, the acreage charge and the CO_2 charge are deductible for the corporate tax and the special surtax. Although high relative to other industries, the effective tax burden is not out of line with the rates of taxation observed in other gas and oil production areas in the world.

The impact on the mainland economy

Given the sheer size of the off-shore petroleum sector, its impact on the mainland economy is bound to be substantial. In 1984/85, when the oil price reached its historical peak, offshore petroleum activities amounted to almost one-fifth (18 per cent) of overall GDP and one-third (35 per cent) of exports. Despite the fall in the oil price in 1986, such GDP, production and export shares were broadly maintained in the second half of the 1980s and the early 1990s, due to

Table 14. **Government's receipts from petroleum activities**

NKr Billion

	1980	Period averages			1993	1994
		1985-86	1987-89	1990-92		
A. Taxes	18.6	41.2	14.6	27.9	26.7	24.6
of which:						
Corporate tax and VAT	9.9	19.6	5.7	11.7	6.4	–
Special surtax	5.0	11.5	1.9	6.3	9.5	–
Royalties	3.6	10.0	6.8	8.5	7.9	–
Acreage charge	0.1	0.2	0.2	0.5	0.6	–
CO, charge	0.0	0.0	0.0	0.9	2.3	–
B. Dividends from Statoil	0.0	1.0	0.3	1.2	1.3	1.1
C. Net revenues from SDFI[1]	0.0	–14.6	–6.3	5.6	0.2	–0.3
A + B + C. Total "net cash flow"	18.6	27.6	8.5	34.7	28.2	25.4
D. National Accounts adjustments[2]	–	6.8	8.5	5.7	16.1	18.0
A + B + C + D. Total revenues	–	34.4	17.0	40.4	44.3	43.4
As per cent of mainland GDP	–	8.5	3.2	7.2	7.3	6.8

1. State's Direct Financial Interest; operating profits less gross investment.
2. Net investment through the SDFI.
Source: Ministry of Finance.

substantial increases in petroleum extraction. Reflecting the high degree of capital intensity, fixed capital formation by the offshore petroleum sector constitutes an even larger portion of total business investment in Norway, representing almost 10 per cent of mainland GDP since the early 1980s (although investment on the NCS was considerably lower in the years following the drop in oil prices in 1986). The rate of return on offshore petroleum investment is comfortably high – about twice the level in manufacturing. The revenues from petroleum extraction thus represent a true "rent" to the Norwegian economy,[47] the bulk of which is reaped by the government (see above).

Apart from arithmetically adding to overall GDP, the petroleum activities also affect the mainland economy through investment spending and intermediate demand.[48] Indeed, about half the demand for goods and services by the offshore petroleum sector is delivered by Norwegian firms, notwithstanding the fact that bidding is entirely open to companies located abroad. As a result, in addition to the 23 000 people employed in 1993 in the petroleum sector off-shore,

57 000 people were working in petroleum-related activities on the mainland, in areas like construction and maintenance of platforms, vessels and landing facilities, as well as logistic and catering services. Moreover, the opportunities offered by the petroleum sector have allowed workers and firms on the mainland to build up considerable know-how in these areas. This has had a favourable impact on Norway's international competitiveness, further contributing to the development of the mainland economy.

On the other hand, petroleum production has "crowded out" export-oriented and import-competing mainland activities, whose share in GDP declined from 27 per cent in 1970 to 14 per cent in 1993 (Figure 25, Panel A). The economic mechanisms which produce such crowding out – known as the "Dutch disease" – reflect the fact that exports of petroleum products tend to boost the exchange rate, public and private spending as well as inflation.[49] As a result, traditional industries exposed to international competition become less competitive and lose market shares both abroad and at home. In Norway such effects were particularly strong in the 1970s, when, indeed, manufacturing industries experienced a dramatic increase in relative unit labour cost in a common currency (Figure 25, Panel B). By contrast, domestic-oriented industries which are "sheltered" from international competition (by nature or through trade protection) have in fact benefited from the increases in domestic demand.

Apart from such structural demand and supply effects, the volatility in petroleum output and prices has tended to accentuate the business cycle in the mainland economy. More particularly, the coming on stream of new oil finds in the early 1970s coincided with a period of economic strength and the 1973/74 oil shock. As a result, the Norwegian mainland economy kept booming and showed signs of overheating during the 1970s, while most European economies went into a protracted period of stagnation. Although the situation normalised in the late 1970s after a currency devaluation and a wage and price freeze, the oil-price and US dollar hikes in the early 1980s again magnified a nascent upturn in the mainland economy, culminating in an unsustainable consumption boom in the mid-1980s. The ensuing downturn, with its climax in a crisis in the financial industry (see Chapter II), was exacerbated by the impact of the steep fall in the oil price in the winter of 1985/86. Conversely, the recovery of the mainland economy which started in 1992 has been reinforced by enhanced activity in the oil and gas sector (see Chapter I).

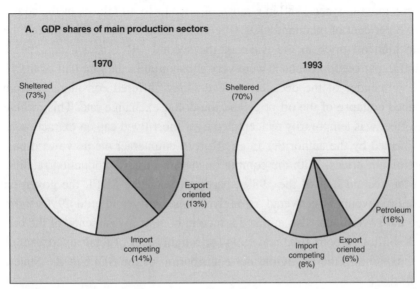

A. GDP shares of main production sectors

1970

Sheltered (73%)

Export oriented (13%)

Import competing (14%)

1993

Sheltered (70%)

Petroleum (16%)

Import competing (8%)

Export oriented (6%)

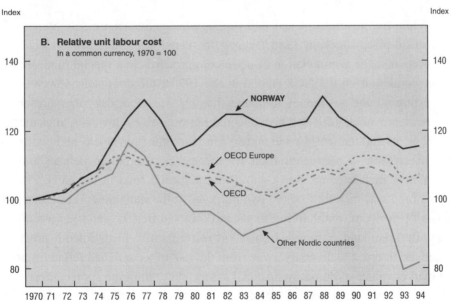

Index

B. Relative unit labour cost
In a common currency, 1970 = 100

NORWAY

OECD Europe

OECD

Other Nordic countries

Index

Source : Statistics Norway; OECD, *Quarterly National Accounts.*

63

The volatility of price and volume movements in the petroleum sector is also reflected in the general government budget, with the State's oil and gas proceeds moving since 1980 in a range of NKr 15 to 40 billion, or the equivalent of 3 to 8 per cent of mainland GDP (Figure 26, Panels A and B).[50] Indeed, helped by the high oil price in the wake of the second OPEC shock and the strong US dollar, petroleum revenues were very substantial in the first half of the 1980s. In the remainder of the decade, however, they suffered considerably from the combined collapse of the oil price and the dollar exchange rate. This mechanical price effect was temporarily exacerbated by a short-lived cap on extraction levels, implemented by the authorities in an effort to counteract the downward pressure on petroleum prices. With the coming on stream of new production facilities set up in the second half of the 1980s, partly through the SDFI, the government's petroleum revenues recovered strongly in the early and mid-1990s.[51] In this period the government also initiated a second bout of investments, of the order of NKr 20 billion in both 1993 and 1994 (or roughly half of total investment on the NCS), explaining the negligible net contribution of the SDFI to the State revenues in those years.

While the government had built up significant financial assets prior to the adverse oil-price shock in 1986 (Figure 26, Panel C), it has been reluctant to institutionalise the accumulation of petroleum proceeds in a special fund. Indeed, when production on the NCS started in the 1970s, the dominant view was that reinvesting oil and gas money in financial assets was more risky than preserving the petroleum stock itself and hence would not be viable. However, after the two OPEC crises and the world-wide increase in real returns on stocks and bonds, the idea of creating a petroleum fund re-emerged in the public debate, and the government in fact considered establishing a special fund in the early 1980s.[52] Such a fund was thought to serve two purposes at the same time: *i)* as a means to transmit petroleum wealth to future generations (see Box 2); and *ii)* as a buffer to shield the mainland economy from short-run volatility in petroleum proceeds. Moreover, in order to diversify away from the risk of a combined fall in oil prices and market values of domestic financial assets and to limit the appreciation of the currency, such a fund was expected to invest primarily in *foreign* assets.[53] The accumulation of assets in the fund of up to NKr 1 trillion (around 140 per cent of mainland GDP) was considered as necessary and realistic at the time. While the

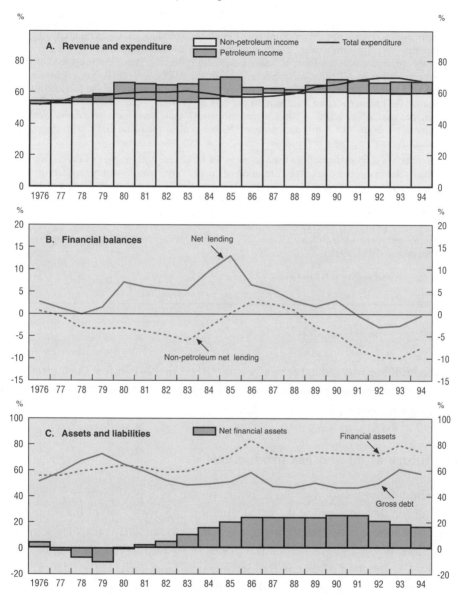

Figure 26. **PETROLEUM REVENUES
AND GENERAL GOVERNMENT FINANCES**

As a percentage of mainland GDP

A. Revenue and expenditure

Non-petroleum income   Total expenditure
Petroleum income

B. Financial balances

Net lending

Non-petroleum net lending

C. Assets and liabilities

Net financial assets   Financial assets

Gross debt

Source: OECD, *Quarterly National Acounts* and OECD Secretariat.

65

Petroleum Fund was indeed formally established in 1991, it remained empty due to the wish to pursue expansionary fiscal policies to combat the recession and rising unemployment (see Chapter II).

The future of oil and gas production

The future evolution of the activities on the NCS is of great importance for the long-run development of the fiscal situation in Norway and of the economy at large. Since these activities started, the government regularly presented long-term projections of oil and gas output and prices in its Long-Term Programmes (and also in a number of National Budgets) which have provided guidance to the authorities in this regard. So far, however, the projections of petroleum output incorporated in these documents typically turned out to be too pessimistic (Figure 27, Panel A). By contrast, projections of oil prices proved to be too

Figure 27. **PROJECTED AND ACTUAL
PETROLEUM OUTPUT AND PRICES**

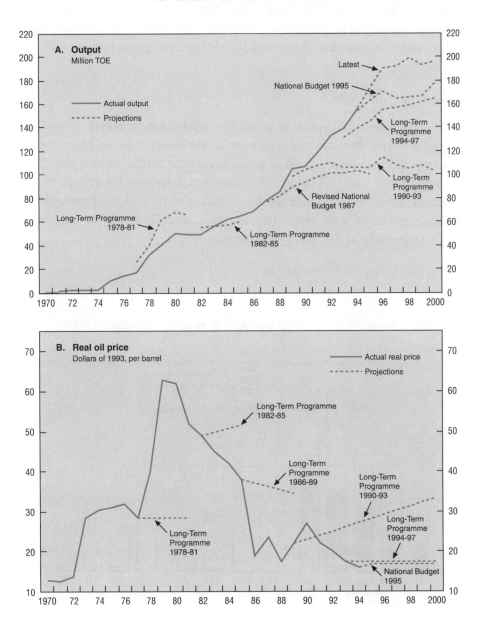

Source: Long-Term Programme, National Budget, various issues.

optimistic (Figure 27, Panel B). These "forecasting errors" point to major uncertainties in this field and imply that future projections will have to be assessed cautiously. The paragraphs below discuss the reasons for these uncertainties and evaluate the latest official long-term projection against that background.

Technology and costs

The persistent underestimation of the production potential of the NCS reflects the gradual but substantial increase in the *recovery factor* (the amount of oil and gas that can be produced in proportion to the total estimated stock) over time. Indeed, the total upgrading of the estimated recoverable resources since production started has *exceeded* the total amount of oil and gas produced, such that the estimates of remaining resources have actually grown in the last two decades (especially in the North Sea, see Figure 28).

Figure 28. **OFFICIAL ESTIMATES OF PETROLEUM RESOURCES OVER TIME**

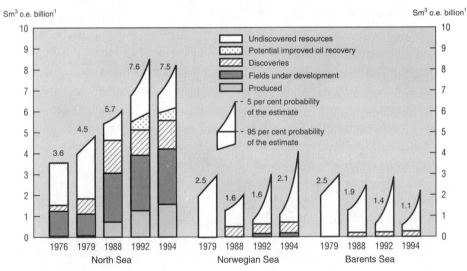

1. Standard cubic meters of oil equivalents.
Source: Petroleum Directorate.

Behind such an enhanced recovery factor lies important progress in technology. Three technological developments in particular have contributed to upward revisions in recoverable resources:

- the introduction of new methods of *geological mapping* (such as computer-based three-dimensional mapping), which have led to more reliable predictions of the exact size, location and chemical composition of undiscovered oil and gas fields. This technique has increased the accuracy of exploratory drilling, and considerably reduced its cost;
- new drilling techniques, which have resulted in significant reductions in production cost and a higher recovery factor for smaller fields. Major progress in this respect results from so-called "horizontal" drilling techniques, which allow one production platform to develop several surrounding small fields at the same time, without having to be moved to other locations. New platform technology has also made it possible to drill on much deeper and hostile waters than initially envisaged;
- another new technique is the injection of natural gas in oil fields to maintain pressure while they are being developed, the gas being recuperated afterwards. This technique became possible with the development of the giant Troll field which contains an enormous reservoir of relatively easily recoverable natural gas (formerly sea water was used for this purpose).

Apart from technical progress, the development of the NCS has benefited considerably from the presence of an extensive network of production platforms and pipelines. The main body of this network was set up in the period when oil prices were still very high, and now largely represents "sunk costs". In combination with the improved technology, the existing infrastructure has made the NCS a less expensive offshore production area than might be expected given its geographical location. In fact, despite "hostile" waters, production costs on the NCS are broadly comparable to those in *e.g.* the Gulf of Mexico, with production cost per barrel averaging US$8.25. However, reflecting the great diversity of fields on the NCS in terms of size and location, costs vary from US$1 to 2 on the Ekofisk field to US$10 to 15 per barrel on recently discovered (typically smaller) fields.

These cost data suggest that the estimated size of recoverable resources on the NCS is highly dependent upon variations in the oil price. A fall in the oil price from its present US$19 per barrel to, for example, US$10 per barrel would

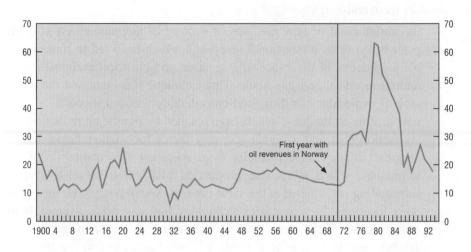

Figure 29. **THE PRICE OF CRUDE OIL SINCE 1900**
Dollars of 1993, per barrel

Source: Oljenindustriens landsforening, Norway.

wipe out substantial recoverable resources, as many of the smaller fields would no longer be profitable. Hence, given the uncertainties related to the future oil price, there is also a substantial risk attached to projections of future oil and gas production (with gas prices largely linked to oil prices). This risk is currently considered to be two-sided. On the one hand, oil prices may be boosted by the global economic recovery, and in fact recent trends point to such a possibility. On the other hand, political developments such as an eventual lifting of the UN embargo against Iraq would exert a downward impact on prices. In any case, a return to the levels of the early 1980s is regarded as unlikely, as the price hikes in the preceding decade appear to have been a unique sequence of events in history (Figure 29).

Uncertain global energy markets

In terms of how global demand and supply developments determine the size of the activities on the NCS, oil and gas are two very distinct products. Aggregate output of *crude oil* on the NCS is largely determined by global price developments in relation to the production cost of the "marginal" field, with global demand and supply factors, as noted above, exerting an indirect impact through variations in the oil price. Moreover, not only the size, but also the *composition* of global demand and supply matters for price developments, as illustrated by the fact that the premium on North Sea crude has disappeared due to global over-supply of the light grades predominant on the NCS. By contrast, output of *natural gas* is largely determined by Norway's success in concluding long-term delivery contracts, such contracts being necessitated by the absence of a significant spot market (as exists for oil) and the long pay-back period of investments in gas-transportation networks. Since natural gas will have to capture an increasing share of Norwegian petroleum production in the future (see above), the willingness of potential users to be engaged in very-long contracts (usually 20 years) is decisive for the future development of the NCS.

One of the main uncertainties in this regard relates to the future supply of natural gas by competing producers present on the European market, Russia and Algeria in particular. Both these producers are connected to the European gas transportation network and are in fact very close to this market (Figure 30). These countries, moreover, possess huge natural gas resources, with Russian stocks amounting to as much as thirty times the Norwegian ones. Another risk is implied by a possible dismantling of national monopolies for gas purchase and supply in EC countries and its potentially negative impact on gas prices from the point of view of gas producers. The fact that Norway has decided not to join the European Union has increased this risk, as the country will not be able to influence the relevant decision making process.

Long-run projections

While subject to the many uncertainties discussed above, official projections for the long term suggest that the total production on the NCS will peak at around 200 million TOE in 1998 in the wake of major investments in new production capacity in recent years, before falling gradually to some 90 million TOE by the year 2030 (Figure 31, Panel A). The projected decline after 1998 is attributable to the maturing of the major oil fields discovered in the 1970s and early 1980s, with few big finds since then. As a result, future output will have to rely progressively on smaller (and more expensive) oil fields and on the still substantial natural gas resources. As noted, both future gas production and the development of small oil fields is subject to uncertainties related to developments in the global energy market.

Figure 30. **GAS RESOURCES AND TRANSPORTATION DISTANCES IN EUROPE**

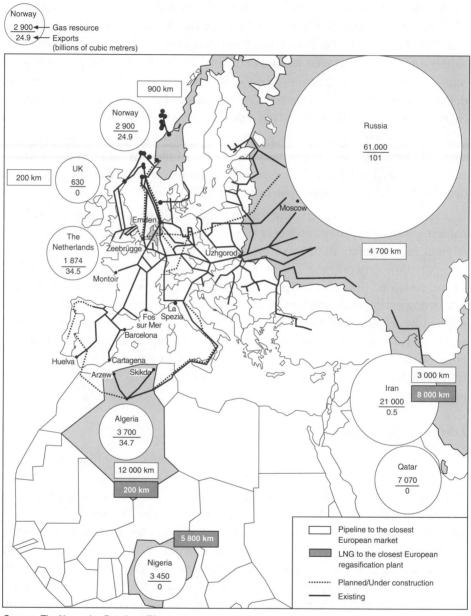

Source: The Norwegian Petroleum Directorate.

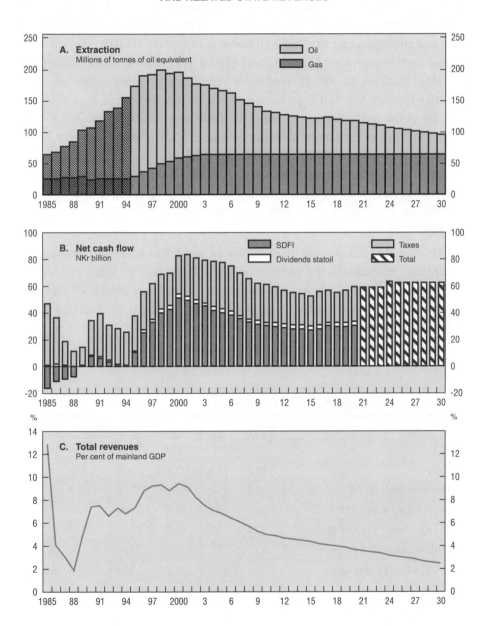

Figure 31. **PROJECTED PETROLEUM EXTRACTION
AND RELATED STATE REVENUES**

A. Extraction
Millions of tonnes of oil equivalent

Oil
Gas

B. Net cash flow
NKr billion

SDFI
Dividends statoil
Taxes
Total

C. Total revenues
Per cent of mainland GDP

Source: Statistics Norway and Ministry of Industry and Energy.

On the basis of these output projections and assuming fixed real energy prices as of 1995, State's revenues from petroleum activities are projected to peak in the year 2001 at around NKr 80 billion – almost twice the estimated level in 1995 and corresponding to almost 10 per cent of mainland GDP – followed by a gradual decline thereafter (Table 15 and Figure 31, Panels B and C). The bulk of the initial increase in the government's petroleum revenues relate to its own activities through the SDFI, reflecting the large investments in new production facilities in the past. In terms of mainland GDP shares, official projections point to a gradual fall in petroleum revenues beyond 2003, down to 6 per cent by 2010 and to 2½ per cent by 2030. This profile largely corresponds to the projected decline in petroleum output, with the impact of lower profit margins of natural gas production (compared to oil production) largely offset by lower production cost owing to technological progress and greater reliance on the existing infrastructure.

In sum, the NCS will unquestionably remain a considerable source of government revenues in the coming decades. However, the dependence of the NCS upon uncertain developments in global oil and gas markets is not to be ignored. Indeed, it would seem wise not to plan on "pleasant surprises" at this stage. The projected gradual fall in output on the NCS and the associated decline

Table 15. **Government's future petroleum revenues**

NKr Billion

	1995	1996	Period averages			
			1997-99	2000-03	2004-20	2021-30
A. Taxes	25.5	28.3	25.8	30.6	27.3	–
B. Dividends from Statoil	1.6	1.7	2.1	2.3	2.3	–
C. Net revenues from SDFI[1]	10.6	25.7	38.9	48.4	32.1	–
A + B + C. Total "net cash flow"	37.7	55.7	66.9	81.3	61.7	62
D. National Accounts adjustments	11.1	5.4	1.4	–7.5	–	–
A + B + C + D. Total revenues	48.8	61.1	68.2	73.9	–	–
As per cent of mainland GDP	7.3	8.8	9.1	8.6	5.0	3.0

1. State's Direct Financial Interest.
2. Net investment through the SDFI.
Source: Ministry of Finance.

in government revenues after the turn of the century may well materialise. If so, this would imply a serious constraint for fiscal policy in the long run, coming on top of budgetary pressure induced by demographic developments. The next section illustrates this aspect.

Long-term constraints on fiscal policy

As most other OECD countries, Norway will experience a rapid ageing of the population in the next decades, with a sharply increasing proportion of people relying on income compensation through public pensions. This tendency is further accentuated by the sharp increase in female labour-market participation in the 1970s and 1980s, which will boost future pension entitlements beyond those emanating from pure demographic trends. The future evolution of public finances crucially depends upon these developments, and it would thus seem relevant to explore how these might evolve. While such an exercise unavoidably relies on tentative assumptions and may contain speculative elements, it should be borne in mind that the demographic patterns for the coming three decades are, to a large extent, already determined. The calculations presented below strongly support the conclusion that the financing of the public pension system may well complicate the sustainability of public finances in the future.

The public pension system

A key feature of the Norwegian public pension system – which is administered by the comprehensive National Insurance Scheme (NIS; see Table 16) – is its broad coverage, with the scheme providing both *basic* pensions for all residents and earnings-related *supplementary* pensions for people with an employment history. Such a combination of two types of provisions in one scheme is not uniformly applied in the OECD area, as in many countries the government grants mainly basic coverage with the bulk of earnings-related coverage being provided by occupational (industry-wide or company-based) schemes in the private sector. Occupational (mainly company-based) schemes exist in Norway as well, but their scope is mostly limited to "topping-up" the income compensation received from the State from around 55 per cent of last-earned income (for a full pension, before tax) to a range of 60 to 70 per cent. Moreover, unlike in some other OECD countries (*e.g.* Finland, the Netherlands), member-

Table 16. **The National Insurance Scheme**
1993

	Beneficiaries		Disbursements	
	Absolute amount	Per cent of population	Billion Krone	Per cent of total
Pensions	904 300	21.0	64.7	54
of which:				
Old age	624 000	14.5	–	–
Disability	232 400	5.4	–	–
Survivors	47 900	1.1	–	–
Other income compensation	310 800	7.3	35.4	30
of which:				
Unemployment	149 000	3.5	–	–
Sickness	49 800	1.2	–	–
Rehabilitation	66 000	1.5	–	–
Single parents	46 000	1.1	–	–
Total income compensation	1215 100	28.3	100.1	84
Healthcare and miscellaneous	–	–	18.6	16
All programmes	–	–	118.7	100

	Contributions	
	Per cent of gross earnings	Per cent of total disbursements
Members	–	27
of which:		
Employees	7.8	–
Self employed	10.7	–
Pensioners	3.0	–
Employers	0-14.3[1]	38

1. Differs per region.
Source: Ministry of Health and Social Affairs.

ship of such schemes is not mandatory in the private sector, although important tax incentives ensure fairly broad participation (about 40 per cent of all private-sector employees).

The pension granted by the NIS when an individual claimant enters retirement is fixed according to a legal formula, defining his/her assessed past earnings on which the pension is based (if there is an employment history), the number of contribution years that are taken into account and the way in which entitlements cumulate per year of contribution. A key parameter in this legal formula is the so-called *basic amount* (NKr 39 230 as from 1 may 1995), which corresponds to the basic pension for a person without an employment history and, indirectly, also determines the earnings-related supplement. According to the formula, past earnings are taken into consideration only insofar as these exceed the basic amount prevailing in the year when those earnings are obtained (Table 17).[54] This basic amount is fixed every year by the Parliament, with as a guiding principle that it should grow in proportion to overall nominal wage earnings.[55] This mechanism ensures that both basic pensions and earnings-related supplements keep up with overall earnings.

In addition to old-age retirement pensions, the NIS also provides survivors' and disability pensions, with the level of benefits essentially determined through the same mechanism as described above (Table 17). One key feature of the disability scheme is that the assessed income includes both actual past earnings and *future* earnings foregone, implying that the benefit level depends only to a limited degree upon the length of a claimant's employment history. While disability pensions are strictly speaking not related to old age, around 45 per cent of people in the 65 to 66 age bracket are declared disabled, compared with only 8.5 per cent of people in the 16 to 65 years age group. Indeed, when disability pensions are taken into account, the average effective retirement age is 61 years (six years below the official retirement age of 67).

Judged by the level of income compensation for an average wage earner, Norwegian public pensions do not stand out as particularly generous. Indeed, at around 55 per cent, the average rate of income compensation in the Norwegian public pension system is not high when compared with equivalent schemes in other European countries (Figure 32). Also, when corrected for international differences in the tax treatment of pensioners, the Norwegian system does not appear to be exceptionally advantageous – with the after-tax replacement rate at around 70 per cent for average earners, as compared to about 100 per cent in Italy, Portugal, Spain and Greece and between 70 and 90 per cent in France, Germany and Belgium. However, such compensation rates are calculated for *individuals* rather than for *families*, and hence exclude basic pensions paid to dependent spouses (which do not uniformly exist in other OECD countries).[56] In addition, international comparisons of replacement rates do not correct for the fact that *indexation mechanisms* may differ across countries. As noted, pensions

Table 17. **Pensions provided by the National Insurance Scheme**
1995

	Old age pension	Disability pension	Survivor's pension
Eligibility	Age 67 years (or older in case of deferred retirement).	Working capacity reduced by 50 per cent or more due to illness, injury of defect, also taking into account job opportunities.	Spouse deceased. Age below 67. Married for at least five years or providing for children with the deceased spouse.
Benefits			
A. Basic pension	Basic amount of NKr 39 230 plus supplement for dependent spouse up to 50 per cent of basic amount (means tests applied to supplement). Basic amount is indexed on overall wage growth.	Same as old age pension.	Same as old age pension.
B. Supplementary pension	Fraction/multiple of the basic amount – based upon the annual average number of "pension points" collected during the best 20 years of one's work history, multiplied by the number of insurance years (counted as of 1967, when the system was founded) with a maximum of 40. The number of pension points allocated in any year is determined by the difference between actual earnings and the basic amount in that year (with a reduced weight for earnings exceeding six times the basic amount).	Same as old age pension but earnings and years *after* entering the disability scheme are also counted as insurance years, up to the age of 67.	55 per cent of supplementary old age or disability pension of the deceased spouse.

Source: Ministry of Health and Social Affairs.

Figure 32. **INCOME REPLACEMENT IN PUBLIC PENSION SYSTEMS**[1]

Per cent of assessed earnings

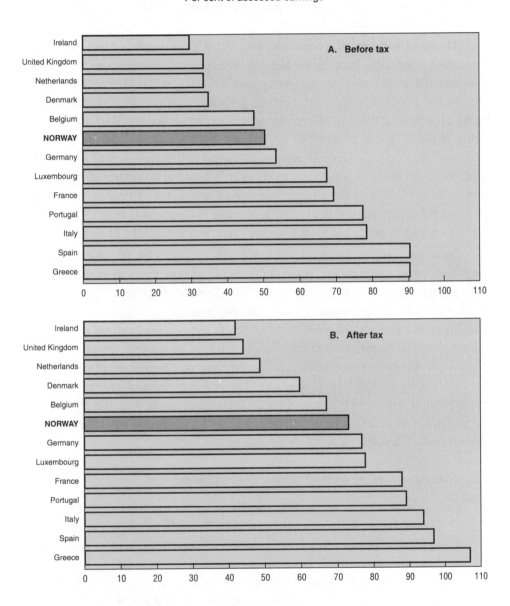

1. Full pension for a person with average earnings, excluding supplements for dependent spouse.
Source: EUROSTAT, *Old age replacement ratios,* Luxembourg 1993; Ministry of Health and Social Affairs, Oslo.

in Norway are indexed on overall nominal earnings, while almost all other OECD countries, with the notable exception of Germany, adjust pensions according to the cost of living.[57]

The total number of people drawing their main income from retirement (including disability) benefits in Norway is broadly comparable to the rest of continental Europe, as is the budgetary cost. In 1993, 900 000 people or 21 per cent of the population received a public pension benefit, with 670 000 persons being allocated an old-age retirement or survivors pension and 230 000 persons being in the disability scheme. In the major OECD economies on the European continent the number of retired persons is also around 20 per cent of the population, while the share of pensioners tends to be considerably smaller in "immigration countries" such as the United States and Canada.[58] At 10 per cent, the ratio of pension benefits-payments to GDP in Norway is comparable to other European OECD countries, while somewhat higher than the overall OECD average.

Since the NIS is financed on a Pay-As-You-Go (PAYG) basis, current contributions to the scheme (essentially State grants) have to match current expenditures. These contributions cover all expenditure of the NIS, including pensions, other income compensation (unemployment, sickness, etc.) and cash benefits to compensate for such items as health care expenditure by individuals. Although social security contributions are paid by employers, employees, self employed and pensioners, these accrue to the State and are not legally earmarked for the funding of the NIS (Table 16). The revenues from these contributions correspond to around two-thirds of total expenditure by the NIS. To compensate for geographical differences in economic strength, employers' contributions vary from 0 and 14.3 per cent of the wage bill across regions.

The consequences of demographic developments

Falling birth rates since the 1970s and increased longevity have changed the composition of the Norwegian population and will lead to its progressive ageing. According to national projections, the number of people at retirement age (67 and above) as a percentage of the working-age population (20 to 67) would peak at around 35 per cent in 2040, after a decline from around 25 per cent in 1990 to just above 20 per cent in 2010. Although the ageing of the population is somewhat less pronounced in Norway than in many other OECD countries (Figure 33, Panel A), this development would substantially increase the participation in

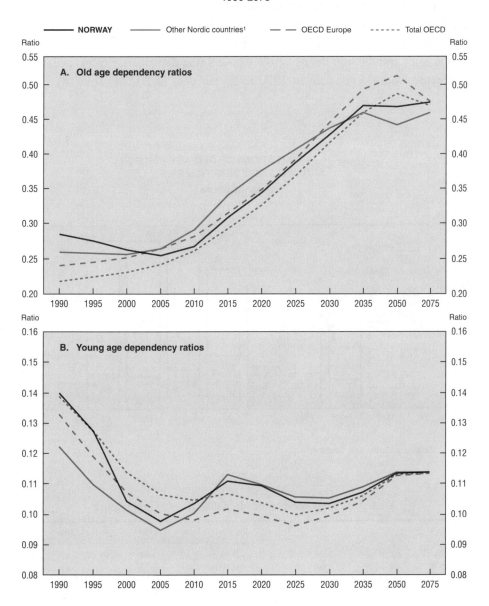

Figure 33. **DEMOGRAPHIC PROJECTIONS**
1990-2075

—— NORWAY   —— Other Nordic countries[1]   — — OECD Europe   - - - - - Total OECD

A. Old age dependency ratios

B. Young age dependency ratios

1.   Denmark, Finland, Sweden.
Source: World Bank.

81

public pension programmes. Indeed, according to national projections, the number of old-age and disability pensioners would rise from around 800 000 in 1990 to 1.3 million by the middle of the next century, with the total population size stabilising (Figure 34).[59] As a result, the ratio between the number of pension beneficiaries and the number of active workers (the dependency ratio) is expected to increase from 44 per cent in 1990 to 53 per cent in 2025 (Table 18).

Figure 34. **PROJECTIONS OF OLD-AGE PENSION AND DISABILITY BENEFICIARIES**
Thousand persons

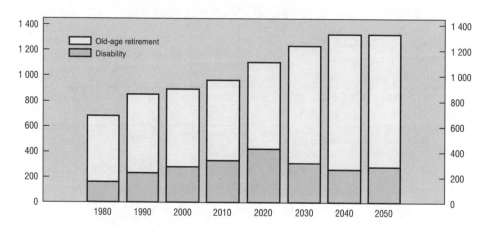

Source: Ministry of Health and Social Affairs.

Table 18. **Long-term trends in public pension expenditure**

	1970	1980	1990	2000	2010	2025
A. Dependency ratio[1]	0.33	0.39	0.44	0.44	0.45	0.53
B. Replacement ratio[2]	0.30	0.33	0.38	0.44	0.49	0.54
A × B. Expenditure ratio[3]	0.10	0.13	0.17	0.19	0.22	0.29

1. Number of pension beneficiaries devided by the number of employed.
2. Average pension benefit per beneficiary divided by average wage earnings per worker.
3. Pension benefits payments devided by total wage earnings.
Source: National Insurance Administration and Statistics Norway.

In addition, a combination of the maturing of pension entitlements[60] and the rapid increase in female participation in the labour market in recent decades will provide a boost to the number of people entitled to earnings-related supplementary pensions. These phenomena are projected to produce a sharp increase in the average pension level per beneficiary, from 38 per cent of average wage earnings in 1990 to 44 per cent in 2000 and 54 per cent in 2025 (Table 18). As a result, the ratio of aggregate pension expenditure to total wage earnings could rise from 17 per cent in 1990 to almost 30 per cent in 2025. It must be noted that Norway is more affected by the increase in participation of women than other Nordic countries. As female participation used to be relatively low compared with these countries until the early-1970s, Norway has gone through a catching-up process since then (Figure 35). Moreover, unlike in other Nordic countries, female participation rates have continued to rise in the 1980s and 1990s, and are expected to rise further in the years to come.

Figure 35. **FEMALE LABOUR FORCE PARTICIPATION**
Per cent of female labour force

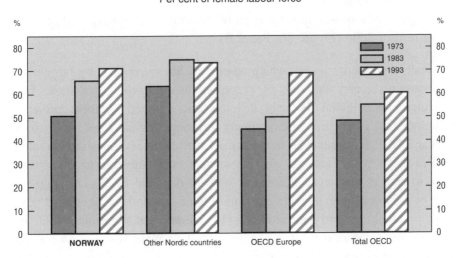

Source: Ministry of Health and Social Affairs.

The implications for public finances

On the basis of the official projections of pension expenditure outlined above, the Secretariat has estimated the implications of demographic developments for overall government expenditure in Norway up to the year 2030. In addition to pension expenditures, another expenditure item susceptible to increases related to the population ageing is *health care*. While no official long-term projections for public health care expenditure are available, this may be expected to rise broadly in line with the old-age dependency ratio (if average cost of medical treatments remain unchanged). Indeed, as has been established in a number of studies, health care costs per individual are typically low below the age of 40 (except in the first year of life), then rise mildly but progressively after the mid-forties and very steeply during the seventies. By contrast, government expenditure on *education* should fall in the early part of the next century, before increasing again somewhat, on the assumption that birth rates will gradually be restored to levels consistent with a stable population size by the year 2030. Secretariat calculations suggest that, after an initial fall, *total* demographically determined expenditure of the government (pensions, health-care and education) would rise from 23 per cent of mainland GDP in 1995 to 33 per cent in 2030 (Figure 36). Assuming, moreover, that all other components of primary (*i.e.* non-interest) expenditure remained constant as a share of mainland GDP, total primary expenditure would increase from 60 per cent of mainland GDP in 1995 to 70 per cent in 2030 (Figure 36, Panel B).

Such expenditure levels, which admittedly are surrounded by large margins of uncertainty, carry the risk of becoming unsustainable over time. This is particularly clear given the debt developments implied by these projections. Assuming that *i)* government's primary revenues remain fixed as a share of mainland GDP (at around 55 per cent); *ii)* petroleum revenues develop as outlined in the previous section; *iii)* real interest rates converge to 4 per cent by 2000, to stay at that level afterwards; and *iv)* that real GDP per capita would grow by 1.5 per cent on average per annum,[61] the government's net asset position would first build up, and then deteriorate by 100 per cent of mainland GDP in the third decade of the next century (Table 19).[62] This is the result of an interaction between increasing budget deficits and falling net interest receipts, culminating in a surge in net borrowing.

Figure 36. **LONG-TERM PROJECTION OF PUBLIC FINANCES**
As a percentage of mainland GDP

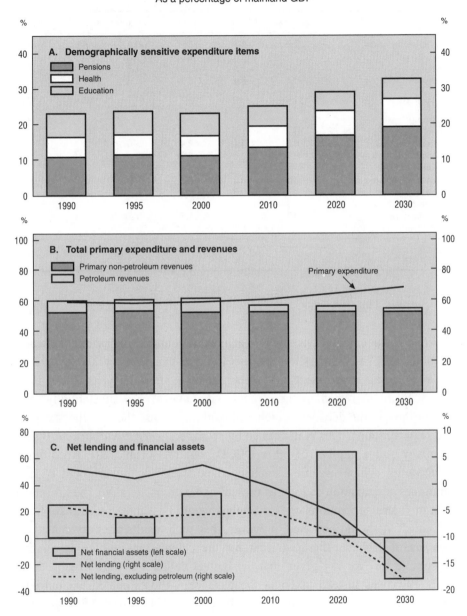

Source: OECD Secretariat.

Table 19. **Public finance in the long run**

Per cent of mainland GDP, period averages

	1986-1990	1991-1995	1996-2000	2001-2010	2011-2020	2021-2030
Primary budget balance	1.9	–2.5	2.0	–0.9	–6.6	–11.5
Net interest receipts	2.0	1.3	0.6	2.6	3.6	0.9
Net lending	3.9	–1.2	2.6	1.7	–3.0	–10.6
Excl. petroleum proceeds	–0.3	–8.4	–6.3	–5.0	–7.3	–13.6
Net financial assets [1]	25.5	15.8	33.3	69.7	63.9	–32.2
Main assumptions						
Pension expenditure	10.7	11.3	11.2	12.2	15.3	18.2
Petroleum proceeds	4.2	7.1	8.9	6.6	4.3	3.0
Mainland GDP growth	0.4	2.0	2.2	1.8	1.4	1.1
Contributions from:						
Change in unemployment	–0.5	0.0	0.2	0.0	0.0	0.0
Growth in labour force	0.7	0.3	0.5	0.3	–0.1	–0.4
Increase in labour productivity	0.2	1.7	1.5	1.5	1.5	1.5
Real long-term interest rate	6.2	6.1	5	4	4	4

1. End of period.
Source: OECD.

While these calculations suggest a more favourable debt outlook than for some other OECD countries,[63] they also indicate that primary and overall balances of general government may turn negative after the year 2000. If this situation is not corrected in time, taxes will have to rise substantially in the course of the coming decades, which will tend to increase the lifetime tax burden of future generations. This is illustrated by so-called *generational accounts* set up for Norway and a number of other OECD countries (Table 20). According to such accounts, which assume "unchanged policies" on government spending programmes and taxation as long as present generations are alive, the lifetime tax burden of future generations of Norwegians would be almost twice that of those now living.[64] It should be noted, however, that such results are very sensitive to the choice of 1993 as the base year for the calculations, which is relatively unfavourable for Norway given that the budget deficit was still sizeable in that year. If 1995 was instead taken as the base year, the estimated tax burden of future versus present generations would be considerably lower. More generally, such calculations are surrounded by wide margins of uncertainty. Nonetheless, Norway does not stand out as a country where high levels of intergenerational

Table 20. **Generational accounts**

Ratio of lifetime tax burdens of future and present generations

	Discount rate 3 per cent		Discount rate 5 per cent	
	Males	Females	Males	Females
Norway	**1.82**	**1.82**	**1.55**	**1.54**
Sweden	1.17	1.17	1.31	1.32
United States	1.94	1.95	2.01	1.99
Germany	1.23	1.23	1.27	1.27
Italy	4.08	4.25	5.45	5.47

Source: OECD Economic Outlook 57, Paris, June 1995.

equity are secured, in spite of the presence of a sizeable petroleum wealth. Hence the need to maintain a tight fiscal stance to ensure sustainable public finances in the long run (see below).

The policy response

Recent initiatives

In various official documents, the government has reiterated its determination to maintain a policy strategy geared towards solidarity and an equitable distribution of economic resources between all strands of Norwegian society. To this end a number of initiatives have been adopted or planned recently, ensuring that: *i)* the State's revenues from oil and gas production remain substantial; *ii)* a significant part of the State's revenues from activities on the NCS be saved for the future; and *iii)* the National Insurance Scheme be maintained and its future funding secured.

The regulatory framework governing activities on the NCS is in the process of being redesigned in view of the constraints arising from the need to develop smaller fields and to shift from oil to gas production.[65] Indeed, given that new production fields tend to be considerably smaller than those previously developed, the government has put forward proposals to change the regulatory framework on the occasion of the 15th licensing round starting this year. These changes focus, in particular, on increasing the shares of individual companies in each license, implying a smaller number of licensees and a smaller share of

Statoil (and the SDFI) – which acknowledges the fact that the shares to be allocated to private companies would otherwise become too small to be profitable. In order to encourage the development of gas fields, the royalty on products other than oil was abolished in 1992. Moreover, as noted, since 1993 the negotiations of gas contracts and their allocation across fields and licensees have been co-ordinated by the Gas Negotiation and Supply Committees.

In the 1995 Revised National Budget, the government re-emphasised the future role of the *Petroleum Fund,* reiterating its wish to build up financial assets as a means to preserve the wealth emanating from the petroleum sector. As a result, the government decided to transfer money to the Petroleum Fund as of 1996. The transfer is provisionally estimated at NKr 10 billion in 1996, but no amount is specified for later years. Investments through the fund should be oriented towards financial assets. The use of the fund for financing investment in *real* assets – such as infrastructure – is not being considered, as the associated returns are deemed to be low and would have to be reaped mostly through taxation and user charges.

The ageing of the population and the associated increase in government expenditure are generally acknowledged to pose problems in the coming decades. As reiterated in a recent White Paper on the future of the social security system,[66] the official policy aims at maintaining the universal National Insurance Scheme in its present form, while its funding should be ensured through enhanced labour-market participation and the reduction in the number of benefit claimants. This policy line, denoted as ''the working approach'', focuses on a reduction in the number of claims for disability benefits and an associated increase in the effective retirement age from 61 at present to a target of 64. After the eligibility rules for disability were tightened in 1991, the number of claimants indeed edged down.[67] New initiatives concentrate on reining in long-term sick leave, which typically precedes a disability claim. To this end special teams have been set up by the local offices of the National Insurance Scheme, the employment offices and the local health services, monitoring each individual case and preparing proposals as to whether a person should have further medical treatment and/or should participate in the new occupational rehabilitation programme. Since this new approach was implemented in July 1993, the number of people on long-term sick leave and disabled has fallen, although this has been at the expense of an increase in the persons enrolled in the rehabilitation programme.

The need for further action

The Secretariat's simulations presented above, which include the estimated impact of the policy initiatives just reviewed, suggest that the reforms of the public pension scheme accomplished so far may not be sufficient to generate sustainable public finances in the long run. Moreover, despite the recent announcement to "activate" the Petroleum Fund, a comprehensive long-run strategy *combining* the management of the petroleum wealth and safeguarding the public pension scheme is yet to be formulated. In this regard, it may be helpful to indicate what fiscal targets such a strategy could seek to attain and how it might be shaped.

A possible strategy, which the government has advocated in the recent White Paper on social security referred to above, would be to proceed in the direction of reducing the cost of the public pension system by raising the effective retirement age. This could take the form of introducing tax incentives for deferred retirement and, more generally, diminishing the favourable tax treatment of pension income. Increased efforts to limit the number of disability beneficiaries would also be desirable in this regard. Simulations by the OECD Secretariat (Table 21) suggest that, in order to establish sustainable public finances in the long run, such reforms would require a decline in public pension expenditure by 1½ per cent of mainland GDP in the second decade of the next century and by 3½ per cent in the third decade. This would represent a downsizing of the level of this category of spending by around one-fifth compared with the baseline projection, on top of the medium-term fiscal consolidation assumed in the projection (see Table 19). The associated budget surpluses would culminate in a financial asset position of the government of around 90 per cent of mainland GDP by the year 2020 (Figure 37), with its net borrowing requirement reaching on average 3 per cent of mainland GDP in the third decade of the next century.

As recently suggested by the central bank, an alternative approach could be to allow the government to build up substantial net financial assets, to cover the liabilities emanating from future pension financing requirements.[68] Ideally, the accumulation of such additional funds should start immediately and continue in the period 2001-10, when both the old-age and the young-age dependency ratios fall below their present levels (Figure 33) and petroleum revenues are still important. According to OECD Secretariat calculations (Table 21), this would require the government balance to remain in surplus in the period 2001-10, which

Table 21. **Alternative scenarios for public finances**

Per cent of mainland GDP, period averages

	2001-2010	2011-2020	2021-2030	Changes from base line[1]		
				2001-2010	2011-2020	2021-2030
Reduced pension expenditure						
Primary budget balance	–0.6	–5.1	–7.9	0.3	1.5	3.6
Net interest receipts	2.6	4.3	4.9	0.0	0.7	4.0
Net lending	2.0	–0.8	–3.0	0.3	2.2	7.6
Excl. petroleum proceeds	–4.6	–5.0	–6.1	0.3	2.2	7.6
Net financial assets[2]	73.6	94.3	93.5	3.9	30.4	125.7
Additional funding						
Primary budget balance	1.2	–6.6	–11.5	2.1	0.0	0.0
Net interest receipts	3.4	6.7	8.5	0.8	3.4	7.6
Net lending	4.5	0.1	–3.0	2.8	3.1	7.6
Excl. petroleum proceeds	–2.1	–4.1	–6.0	2.8	3.1	7.6
Net financial assets[2]	103.1	146.0	164.2	36.4	82.1	196.4

1. See Table 19.
2. End of period.
Source: OECD.

Figure 37. **GOVERNMENT'S NET FINANCIAL ASSETS**
As a percentage of mainland GDP

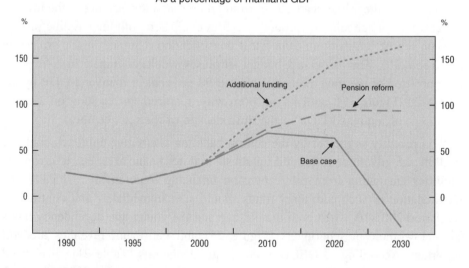

Source: OECD Secretariat.

90

would imply a fiscal consolidation of around 2 per cent of mainland GDP compared to the base line scenario presented in Table 19. The amount of financial assets which would thus be accumulated by the government could reach a level of 160 per cent of mainland GDP by 2030 (Figure 37).

The advantages of building up financial assets that way would be the following:

– *first*, this approach would provide the government with an instrument to increase investments abroad in order to relieve upward pressure on the krone and the associated "crowding out effects". As noted, such an investment strategy would also be recommendable from a viewpoint of risk diversification away from too large a dependence of the economy on the petroleum sector;
– *second,* the accumulation of financial assets by the government represents public saving, and as such also contribute to national savings;
– *third,* the financial assets could be used to shield the government account from volatility in petroleum revenues, thereby smoothing the business cycle of the mainland economy.

However, while contributing to sustainable public finances in the long run, such an approach might incur the risk of generating political pressure to spend the accumulated funds on public goods and services. One way for the government to reduce this risk would be to make a clear commitment to use the assets to be accumulated for the financing of future pension expenditure, in effect implying a move from pay-as-you-go financing toward partial or full funding of the public pension system.[69] This would also imply a more equitable burden-sharing between generations.

A third option, which so far has not attracted much attention in the Norwegian public debate, would be to cut back the accumulation of earnings-related pension entitlements under the NIS, while obliging workers to build up equivalent resources in private occupational schemes. This would make the system closer to those in countries like the United Kingdom, the Netherlands and Finland. Greater emphasis on occupational pension schemes would enhance the actuarial fairness of old-age income provisions, as such schemes typically establish a link between contributions and benefits for each individual participant. In addition, an increased reliance on occupational pension schemes would allow

Table 22. **Legal ceilings on investments by occupational pension funds**

Per cent of total assets

	Foreign assets	Re-investment in own company	Securities of a single issuer	All securities	*Memorandum item:* minimum in government securities
Norway	–	25	–	20	–
Belgium	–	15	5	–	15
Denmark	–	–	2	60[1]	–
Finland	–	–	–	–	–
Germany	5	–	–	–	–
Netherlands	–	10	–	–	–
Portugal	–	10	–	10	–
Spain	–	–	10	–	–
United Kingdom	–	5	–	–	–

1. Including deposits.
Source: Clifford Chance, Pensions in Europe, 1993.

them to become more prominent as institutional investors, which might favour a broadening of the Norwegian capital market. For this to materialise, however, the legal ceiling on investments in securities of 20 per cent of a funds' portfolio – one of the most constraining regulations among European countries (Table 22) – would need to be modified. As well, legislation would have to ensure portability of pension entitlements from one company/industry to another.

To sum up, although government petroleum revenues are expected to rise in the medium run, relying on further increases in such income to offset the rising cost of the public pension scheme in the next century would not be appropriate. Hence the need to further consolidate the budget in a way that would ensure the funding of public pensions beyond the end of the present decade. One option in this regard would be to reduce pension expenditure by increasing the effective retirement age. This would have the advantage of maintaining the pension system in its present form – in line with the recommendation of a recent government White Paper on the issue. Alternatively, the government could be allowed to build up financial assets, with the return on these assets being used for future pension financing requirements. A third option would be to gradually shift the management of earnings-related pensions from the public to the private sector.

V. Conclusions

Growth of Norway's mainland economy posted a ten-year record of nearly 4 per cent in 1994. This performance was driven by a rapid recovery of private demand for durables and dwellings, reflecting significant progress in households' financial consolidation, and by more buoyant manufacturing exports. Mainland business investment also picked up in the second half of 1994, boosted by increased levels of capacity utilisation. These developments led to a marked improvement in the labour market, with the rate of unemployment declining to 5½ per cent by early 1995, despite a cyclical rebound in labour force participation. As wage pressure remained subdued, price inflation was kept below 2 per cent, although it has accelerated somewhat recently in response to indirect tax increases. Together with soaring energy exports, higher international commodity prices contributed to maintain a sizeable current account surplus, despite a surge in imports triggered by the stronger domestic demand.

While slowing, the economic upturn is projected to continue, with mainland GDP growing by nearly 3 per cent in 1995 and 2½ per cent in 1996. Overall output growth, including offshore activity, is expected to be stronger due to continued buoyancy of the oil and gas sector, and this could generate a widening of the external surplus. Housing demand might be less strong than in 1994 and capital formation on the Norwegian continental shelf is likely to fall, partly offset by the revival of mainland business investment. While private sector employment is expected to continue to expand rapidly, the reduction in unemployment could be hampered by a further rise in participation rates and some decline in the number of persons enrolled in active labour market programmes. Wage growth, nonetheless, may accelerate towards the end of the projection period, in the face of improved labour market conditions and corporate profitability. This could provoke stronger inflation pressure – the more so if domestic demand growth does not subside as projected.

In such an environment, prudent macroeconomic management is warranted. For more than two years, monetary policy has proved relatively easy by historical standards, helped by the remarkably stable exchange rate since the floating of the currency in December 1992. Indeed, short-term interest rates have mostly remained around 5½ per cent since early 1994, with the differential against German rates at 100 basis points most recently. Moreover, after falling substantially in the early stage of the recovery, long-term rates have subsequently risen by less than in other OECD countries, with bond yields at roughly 7¾ per cent in April 1995. By reducing the number of bankruptcies, and in turn the volume of loan losses, these developments have considerably helped strengthen banks' balance sheets. As a result, fears of credit supply constraints following the banking crisis of the early 1990s have been removed.

The decision to let the krone float has not fundamentally altered the conduct of monetary policy which continues to be geared towards the pursuit of low and stable inflation. Norwegian authorities view the maintenance of a stable exchange rate against European currencies as a key element in this regard, as it offers a clear signal to social partners with respect to wage and price developments. Given this emphasis on exchange rate stability – which has been explicitly reaffirmed by the government in its 1994 Revised National Budget – the scope for monetary restriction to prevent a build-up of inflationary tensions may be limited in the period ahead by the current strength of the Norwegian krone associated with the country's healthy external position.

Consequently, fiscal policy should have a crucial role to play in dampening potential inflation pressure. Indeed, the current fiscal stance is going in this direction, as Norway stands out as a country where significant progress in budget consolidation is being achieved. With oil revenues moving up slightly, the general government balance is expected to turn from a deficit in 1993 and 1994 (of 2 and ¼ per cent of GDP respectively) to a surplus of 1½ per cent in 1995. While in part reflecting the stronger economic activity, increases in indirect taxation as well as restraint in public consumption and income transfers are also contributing to this improvement.

Budget surpluses are officially projected to be maintained during the rest of the decade. This results mainly from the expected increase in the State's petroleum revenues after the sizeable investments in new production facilities which were undertaken on the Norwegian continental shelf in recent years. Norway's fiscal outlook thus compares favourably with those of many other OECD economies, the more so since the public sector enjoys a comfortable net asset position despite the expansionary fiscal stance pursued in the late 1980s and early 1990s to combat the recession and support employment. Nonetheless, the fiscal authorities are faced with a major challenge in the long run, given the foreseeable decline in the oil wealth and the likely increase in welfare expenditure due to ageing population.

As discussed in detail in Chapter IV of the *Survey*, although the prospects for government petroleum revenues currently look favourable, it would be unwise to rely upon further increases in this source of income after the next decade given the uncertainties attached to oil and gas exploitation in the future. Two developments are worth stressing in this respect. *First*, with the major fields now maturing, oil production will focus increasingly on smaller fields which prove more costly and more difficult to exploit despite the huge technical progress accomplished in this domain. *Second*, as oil resources will gradually be depleted, future energy production will be dominated by natural gas, the demand for which is increasing in Europe. However, in this area Norway must count with large competitors (Russia and Algeria). In addition, gas users may become more reluctant to commit to long-term delivery contracts which the Norwegian authorities seek to conclude to justify the required expensive investments in pipelines.

Given these uncertainties, the best option for the authorities in the coming years would be to save a growing portion of oil and gas revenues, for example through the state's petroleum fund created to this effect in 1991, both for intergenerational equity considerations and to better shield the budget from the volatility in energy prices. This orientation, designed to build up financial assets through budget surpluses, would seem to be all the more justified as, in Norway as in many other OECD countries, future budgetary costs related to the financing of public pensions will place a heavy burden on fiscal policy in the next century. Official projections indeed suggest that, with the progressive ageing of the population, the ratio of pension beneficiaries to active workers would rise from 44 per cent in 1990 to 53 per cent in 2025. In addition, the rapid increase in female participation in the labour market over the past twenty years will inevitably boost the number of people entitled to earnings-related supplementary pensions early in the next century. As a result, government pension expenditures are projected by the OECD to pick up from an average of 11 per cent of mainland GDP in the period 1986-95 to more than 18 per cent in 2020-30.

Simulations by the OECD show that, in the absence of offsetting cuts in other categories of expenditure and despite the currently comfortable net asset position and projected fiscal consolidation, such potential pressure on government spending would lead to unsustainable public debt developments in the long run. Hence the need to keep a tight rein on future overall state expenditure. In addition, adjustments in the existing public pension system would be desirable to ensure its funding beyond the end of the present decade. These could include measures to reduce the cost of the system, such as limiting the number of recipients of disability pensions, creating tax incentives for deferred retirement and reducing the favourable tax treatment of pension benefits. An alternative option could be to adopt an overall fiscal stance that would generate higher public savings over the next ten to fifteen years, when government revenues are likely to be strong, so as to cope with the expected increase in ageing related welfare expenditure. This would in effect imply a move from the present pay-as-you-go arrangements toward partial or full funding of the public pension system, without necessarily requiring the institution of any particular new mechanism. Other approaches – such as relying to a greater extent on occupational pension schemes in the private sector than is currently the case – might be considered as well. This would have the advantage of allowing such schemes to become more prominent as institutional investors. Moreover, as private schemes typically establish a link between contributions and benefits for each individual participant, such a move may help promote a more balanced inter-generational distribution of wealth.

More generally, increased emphasis on structural reform is called for, so as to improve the overall efficiency of the mainland economy and strengthen long term prospects for employment. Areas where additional initiatives would seem essential include the labour market, taxation, government subsidies, competition policy and banking. As suggested in last year's *Economic Survey* and in the *OECD Jobs Study*, benefit entitlements of the unemployed in Norway should be reduced in order to enhance work incentives and encourage a better consistency between wage and productivity levels, especially for low-skilled workers. Government policy has recently moved in this direction with a proposed reform of the unemployment insurance system. This will contain an effective limitation of benefit duration, but the impact of this measure will be partly offset by the proposed simultaneous increase in benefits for long-term unemployed. Lowering unemployment income support further would allow the freeing of resources for training and other active labour market programmes, the efficiency of which should, at the same time, be subject to closer scrutiny. In addition, the functioning of the labour market could be improved by easing the currently tight regulation of fixed-term employment contracts and by encouraging a larger degree of wage flexibility to facilitate the recruitment of low skilled workers entering the market.

Some elements of the tax system could also be reviewed. In particular, a reform of the wealth tax would be desirable to treat equally households' investments in real and financial assets, with a view to improving resource allocation through the capital market. Likewise, a reduction of the "tax wedge" between labour compensation and take home pay would be useful as this is generally acknowledged to have favourable effects on employment. More broadly, given the already high overall level of taxation in Norway, consolidating the budget situation should be achieved without further tax increases, which makes strong expenditure discipline essential.

With respect to *agricultural support* – one of the highest among OECD countries – evidence suggests that Norway's social objectives of self sufficiency in food supply and the preservation of rural population in remote areas are currently achieved at a very high cost to the economy at large. Given the misallocation of resources entailed by the existing support scheme, and its drawbacks for consumers, a reduction of the assistance to this sector could bring substantial welfare gains. A rapid implementation of the GATT agreement would constitute a positive step in this direction. As well, apart from shipbuilding – where cuts in subsidies are envisaged as a result of the recent OECD accord in this area – government support to manufacturing remains relatively high and should be streamlined.

In the field of *competition policy*, reforms achieved recently – in particular the reduction of public monopolies in the electricity supply, air transportation, telecommunications, pharmaceutical and grain markets – have helped reduce prices and raise the quality of services provided on these markets. Further action could be taken to separate the remaining natural monopoly activities, such as grid management in the electricity sector, from those now open to free competition. This would facilitate the efforts of the competition authorities in ensuring that monopoly rents of public enterprises are not used to subsidise their market-oriented business.

Finally, as for the *banking industry*, whose profitability has returned to more satisfactory levels, the challenge facing the authorities still remains to create the conditions for a leaner and more efficient financial structure through enhanced competition and rationalisation. Recent progress has been made in this regard, as reflected in significant reductions in staff and branch numbers of most banks. Further improvements would require the pursuit of the gradual return of banks' capital to private ownership, and, as currently considered by the government, a refocus of state bank activities on social objectives (such as housing loans to low-income groups).

In *summary*, growth of the Norwegian economy appears set to continue, albeit at a slower pace, with buoyant exports and increased mainland business investment as main contributing factors. While inflation has remained subdued so far, helped by wage moderation and exchange rate stability, there is nonetheless a risk of the economy overheating if the expansion in domestic demand continues at the same speed. With the scope for monetary restriction likely to be constrained by exchange rate considerations, it is important for fiscal policy to contribute to rein in potential inflation pressure by generating budget surpluses while activity grows strongly. Provided a disciplined approach to public expenditure is maintained, this orientation would also create the scope for cushioning future increases in welfare spending, due to ageing population, when oil revenues start declining. Additional structural reforms – in the labour market in particular – would improve the efficiency of the mainland economy and strengthen its ability to adapt to external shocks.

Notes

1. Estimates provided by the Confederation of Norwegian Business and Industry suggest that the overall rate of return in manufacturing has risen from around 7 per cent in 1992 to 10 per cent in 1994, compared with an average of around 9 per cent in the period 1981-91.

2. In 1994, active labour market programmes absorbed around 2.6 per cent of the labour force.

3. The Labour Force Survey may slightly overestimate the rate of open unemployment, as it counts some participants in labour market programmes as job seekers.

4. As shown in the *Economic Bulletin* of the Bank of Norway 1994/4, Oslo, pp. 273 and 280-283.

5. The Bank of Norway's official rates setting the floor and ceiling for short term money market rates have been unchanged since February 1994 at, respectively, 4.9 and 7 per cent (effective rates).

6. On the forces which caused the crisis, see previous *OECD Surveys*.

7. The increase in the total stock of domestic credit extended to the public can be fully attributed to loans granted to investments in new or existing residences.

8. In Norwegian banks, accrued interest is credited on accounts almost exclusively on 31 December. If average interest rates in a particular year are significantly below those of the previous year, the December year-on-year growth rate of deposits will fall. Such an impact tends to dissipate when clients adjust their bank deposits in subsequent months.

9. As a result, indirect tax proceeds on mainland activities are estimated to have increased by 11 per cent compared with an initial projection of less than 5 per cent.

10. In 1993 and 1994 net lending of the central government was about NKr 23 and 20 billion (3 per cent of GDP) higher than the State budget balance, due to the inclusion in central government net lending of the surplus of the social security funds and the State's direct capital injections (mainly in the oil sector).

11. Without the corrections indicated, the nominal increase is somewhat smaller.

12. This is done by lowering the cap on local government income taxes and increasing the basic rate for State income taxes correspondingly. As local governments are legally required to run (nearly) balanced budgets, the central government can influence spending levels at the local level directly through measures that affect local revenues. As all municipalities at present use the highest rate allowed, changes of the cap has immediate effects on revenues.

13. Participation in an ALMP counts as regular work when assessing the eligibility for benefits. As participation has been granted more or less automatically to persons about to exhaust their benefits entitlement – formally restricted to 80 weeks – very few, if any, unemployed people have until now lost their right to benefits entitlements.

14. See *The OECD Jobs Study*, 1994.

15. OECD, *Employment outlook*, 1993.

16. See *Norges Offentlige Utredninger* (1992:26), "En nasjonal strategi for økt sysselsetting i 1990 årene", Oslo, 1992.

17. In particular, earnings below NKr 900 000 and from NKr 2.9 to NKr 4.9 million are now taxed as wage income, while those from NKr 900 000 to NKr 2.9 million and exceeding NKr 4.9 million are taxed as capital income.

18. Revenues from the government's own petroleum activities are (by definition) not taxed, which artificially reduces the tax burden.

19. See *The OECD Jobs Study*, 1994 and *Taxation, Employment and Unemployment*, OECD, 1995 (forthcoming).

20. A. Brendemoen and H. Vennemo, "Hva koster det å øke skattene", *Økonomiske Analyser* 1993/8, pp. 22-28.

21. At the same time, mortgage interest payments of households continue to be fully deductible for income taxation.

22. *Stortingsmelding nr. 35* (1994-95). See also Chapter IV.

23. A. Dulsrud, "Hvad betyder grensehandel hvis Sverige blir medlem av EU", Statens Institut for Forbrugsforskning, (mimeo) 1994.

24. More attention has also been given to the issue of regulatory costs. In May 1994, a committee with broad representation was established by the government to recommend guidelines on how to assess public and private costs of complying with new regulation. The result of its deliberations will be published at the end of 1995.

25. One could expect that liberalisation would lead to some "cream-skimming" whereby prices are lowered and the number of flights increased on routes where demand for seats is relatively high. This would reduce the airlines' capacity to subsidise less used routes, forcing them to raise prices, and eventually reduce capacity. One reason why this has not happened yet could be that the former monopoly service may have been inefficient, providing room for new and more cost-conscious operators to run profitable services even at lower prices.

26. That part of the Telenor, to operate on fully competitive terms with the private sector, could over time be privatised as there would be no obvious reason for keeping this activity within the public sector.

27. The State has already split up its own electricity activities into *Statnett SF*, a grid manager, and *Statkraft*, an electricity producer.

28. The largest cuts in import tariffs and biggest increases in import quotas apply to goods which are produced only in small quantities in Norway. See Ivar Gaasland, "Konsekvenser for Norge av jordbruksavtalen i GATT", *SNF-rapport* 58/94, September 1994.

29. At 7.8 per cent of GDP (or 14 per cent of general government expenditure), the cost of public health care is one of the lowest among OECD countries. Roughly 85 per cent of health spending is financed by local authorities, mainly through local income taxes. User fees – especially related to dental care, medicine and use of private specialists – account for around 12 per cent of total expenditure.

30. "Samarbeid og styring: Mål og virkemidler for en bedre helsetjeneste", *Stortingsmelding nr. 50.* (1993-94), Department of Social Services and Health.

31. One example quoted in the White Paper was operations on aneurysms on main arteries, which in 1991 were performed fewer than five times in as many as 33 hospitals.

32. These issues are currently treated by the Banking Commission, which over the next year will present a number of reports. The report on deposit insurance is expected in the summer of 1995 while another on Corporate Banking Governance is envisaged to appear in mid-1996.

33. See in particular the *1992/93 Survey* which contains a special chapter on "The Banking Crisis and Financial Reform".

34. Some major Swedish banks have opened up several branches in Norway, focusing on the wholesale market and providing banking services to larger Norwegian firms.

35. The special chapter of the 1992/93 *Survey*, as quoted above, includes an in-depth discussion of the problems arising from public ownership of banks.

36. See for example the Long-Term Programme 1993-97.

37. *Stortingsmelding nr. 41* (1994-95).

38. See Willi Leibfritz, Deborah Roseveare, Douglas Fore and Eckhard Wurzel, "Ageing Populations, Pension Systems and Government Budgets: How do they affect saving?", *Economics Department Working Paper No. 156,* OECD, Paris, 1995.

39. Petroleum normally understood to comprise crude oil, Natural Gas Liquids (NGL's) and dry gas.

40. An initial license of six years is guaranteed, which is renewable for another four years. After that, licensees keep half of the awarded area for another 30 years.

41. Moderate extraction rates were also judged to be conducive to a gradual structural adjustment process from traditional tradeable products to petroleum production.

42. The dividend pay-out is annually decided upon by the Norwegian Parliament.

43. By the end of 1993, Statoil held allotments in 130 production licenses, and was the main operator on five fields.

44. Since then the company has embarked upon production activities in Azerbaijan in co-operation with British Petroleum.

45. *Stortingsmelding nr. 25* (1973-74).

46. Depreciation is linear over six years.

47. This rent was estimated at 13 per cent of GDP in 1984 and at around 4.5 per cent in 1990. The present value of this rent represents the petroleum wealth which is presently estimated at NKr 700 billion (real rate of return 7 per cent). Including the fixed capital on the Norwegian Continental Shelf, the wealth is estimated at NKr 1 000 billion, of which over NKr 800 billion accrues to the State.

48. Intermediate demand by the petroleum sector is of the same order of magnitude of investment demand and amounted to 6.5 per cent of mainland GDP in 1993.

49. See O. Thøgersen, "Economic policy, macroeconomic performance and the Norwegian petroleum wealth, a survey", Norwegian School of Economics and Business Administration and SNF, Bergen, 1994 (mimeo).

50. National Accounts basis, with net investments through the SDFI booked as net lending. As these are considered as expenditure in the State's Budget, budget data differ from the national accounts by this amount, see Table 14.

51. At the initial stage of the SDFI in the 1980s, the net cash flow from it was negative as the state was heavily investing in new production capacity on the NCS, which reduced the state cash flow by the same amount. On a national accounts basis, however, the SDFI contribution was positive, as the investments are considered as financial asset formation (see footnote 50).

52. Tempoutvalgets innstilling, *NOU* 1983:27.

53. Already in 1979 a swap of shares between Volvo and Statoil was considered to this effect. It was rejected by Volvo shareholders, however.

54. The earnings-related supplement is subject to a minimum amount, the so-called special supplement, which is granted to all pension beneficiaries irrespective of their past earnings. The minimum pension (basic pension plus special supplement) thus amounts to NKr 63 376 per year.

55. Since the 1980s, however, the annual upratings of the basic amount have lagged overall nominal wage increases by about 1 percentage point per year.

56. Notwithstanding that the compensation rate for married people is around 5 per cent lower than for single persons.

57. Moreover, international comparisons of this kind are complicated by the fact that many other factors affect the economic well-being of retired people – such as housing allowances and reduced charges for health care.

58. See, for more details, Paul Van den Noord and Richard Herd, "Estimating pension liabilities: a methodological framework", *OECD Economic Studies No. 23*, winter 1994.

59. Concerning disability, these projections assume that inflows of new disability beneficiaries per age and sex group remain constant at their average 1989-93 levels.

60. The NIS being founded in 1967, all beneficiaries will have full entitlements only by 2007.

61. The last assumption is in line with the latest *Long Term programme* which takes as a base line an extension to 2030 of the Employment Commission's "Solidarity Alternative" running from 1992 to 2001. The Solidarity Alternative assumed moderate mainland GDP growth up to 2001 of around 2½ per cent and somewhat lower for over all GDP growth. In the period 1998-2001, employment is projected to grow by 1 per cent, but ¾ per cent in terms of hours worked. The unemployment rate falls to 4½ per cent in 1997 and to 3½ per cent in 2001. The current account improves considerably, implying a reallocation of Norwegian wealth from petroleum reserves to financial assets. The SNA central government deficit falls from 3¼ in 1993 to 2¼ in 1997 (excluding oil 13 and 12 per cent, respectively).

62. The Solidarity Alternative in the Long Term Programme 1994-97 implies a fall in central government financial assets to 0 already by 2000 due largely to the less favourable initial fiscal position in 1995 than in the OECD's calculations.

63. See Willi Leibfritz, Deborah Roseveare and Paul van den Noord, "Fiscal policy, government debt and economic performance", *Economics Department Working Paper No. 144,* OECD, Paris 1994.

64. The calculations for Norway are updates of those presented in A.J. Auerbach, J. Gokhale, L.J. Kotlikoff and E. Steigum, "Generational Accounting in Norway: is Norway overconsuming its petroleum wealth?" July 1993 (mimeo). See also The National Budget for 1995.

65. *Storting White Paper No. 26* (1993-1994), "Challenges and perspectives for petroleum activities on the Norwegian Continental Shelf".

66. *Stortingsmelding nr. 35* (1994-95).

67. The stricter application of criteria for eligibility includes: 1) more stringent demands for rehabilitation of alcohol and drug addicts, 2) the abandon of old age as a reason for disability, 3) tighter conditions regarding geographical and occupational mobility, 4) more stringent sanctions against doctors not conforming rules about sickness certification, rehabilitation and disability pensions.

68. See the "Address by the Governor of the Norges Bank at the meeting of the Supervisory Council of the Bank on 23 February 1995", Norges Bank, *Economic Bulletin* 1995/1, pp. 3-15.

69. It may be worth noting in this context that the government in fact set up a social security trust fund in 1967. It has invested mainly in government bonds and amounted in 1993 to some 10 per cent of GDP (NKr 81.6 billion).

CALENDAR OF MAIN ECONOMIC EVENTS

1993

January

The central bank cuts its "overnight" lending rate twice by ½ percentage point to 10 per cent.

February

The central bank progressively lowers its "overnight" lending rate to 9.25 per cent.

A Government Committee on VAT reforms favours a continuation of the present uni-rate system.

March

The central bank cuts its "overnight" lending rate twice by ¼ percentage point, bringing it down to 8.75 per cent.

The Government Committee, appointed to suggest concrete cuts in transfers totalling NKr 5 billion, is not able to agree on a common proposal for reductions.

Following a writing down of the banks ordinary share capital, Den norske Bank receives a further NKr 1.5 billion from the Government Bank Insurance Fund.

April

The central bank lowers the overnight lending rate in four steps to 7.75 per cent.

Norway's negotiations on EC membership start.

A wage agreement is reached between LO and NHO, as the government commits to provide to private pension schemes NKr 50 million for the lowering of the minimum retirement age. The agreement entails an increase in hourly wages of NKr 1 for workers not concerned by local negotiations and NKr ½ are for workers who may benefit from additional increases through local negotiations. Excluding the effect of local settlements, this amounts to a general wage increase of 1½ to 2 per cent.

May

The revised 1993 Budget is presented to Parliament. The State budget deficit is expected to reach NKr 54 billion in 1993, roughly NKr 5 billion above the level of the draft budget approved in December 1993, reflecting mainly lower revenues from both mainland and oil activities.

The central bank cuts the "overnight" lending rate by ¼ percentage point to 7.5.

June

The Parliament adopts tax reliefs for persons located in the northern regions of Finnmark and Nor-Troms, amounting – for an average income person – to NKr 7 000 to 8 000 per year.

July

Seven leading gas producers sign a contract with German companies, implying an expansion of gas deliveries of 3.5 billion cubic metres per year, and a 10 to 15 per cent price rise.

September

After the general election to Parliament (Storting), the labour party remains in government with strengthened parliamentary representation. The distribution of seats is the following (results from the previous election in 1989 are in brackets): Labour Party 67 seats (63), Centre Party 32 seats (11), Conservatives 28 seats (32), Christian Peoples Party 13 seats (14), Socialist Left Party 13 seats (17), Progressive Party 10 seats (22), Liberals 1 seat (0) and Red Electoral Alliance 1 seat (0).

October

The newly-formed government presents the draft National Budget for 1994. Based upon an oil price of NKr 120 per barrel, the State budget deficit for 1994 is projected at NKr 46.4 billion; excluding oil-related revenues and expenditures the deficit is expected to reach NKr 72.5 billion.

The central bank reduces the "overnight" lending rate by ½ percentage point to 7 per cent.

A coalition of the government and the Christian Peoples Party agree on a formula for implementing an increase in the wealth tax, in line with the draft budget proposal.

November

The central bank cuts the "overnight" lending rate by ¼ percentage point to 6.75 per cent.

In the context of EC negotiations, the Norwegian Government presents a position paper on fishing, with the central tenet that fishing levels north of 62 latitude shall be decided by the Norwegian authorities.

December

The central bank raises the "overnight" lending rate by ¼ percentage point to 7 per cent.

The national budget for 1994 is adopted. Still based upon an oil price of NKr 120 per barrel, the State budget deficit is expected to be NKr 42.6 billion; excluding oil revenues and expenditures, the deficit is projected at NKr 70.3 billion.

1994

January

The EEA agreement comes into force. Representatives of the European Union (EU) and EFTA reach an accord on additional regulations to be included in the EEA agreement, denoted as EEA2.

Statoil reports the first oil discovery in the Barents Sea.

The boards of Norges Postbank and the Postal Giro endorse a proposal to merge the two financial institutions with effect from 1 January 1995.

February

The central banks cuts the "overnight" lending rate by ¼ percentage point to 6.75 per cent.

A government advisory committee presents its report on the future of private pension insurance. It proposes to extend the favourable tax treatment of private pensions to defined contribution schemes (under current regulation only defined benefit schemes qualify for reduced taxation).

April

The government formally proposes to merge Norges Postbank and Postal Giro with effect from 1 January 1995. The new bank will be the fourth largest bank in the country.

The new gas pipeline Zeepipe to transport natural gas from the Troll field to Zeebrugge in Belgium is officially opened.

This year's wage negotiations take place on a union by union basis without guidance from a central settlement. The public sector pay settlement entails a wage increase of NKr 2 100 for both central and local government employees as from 1 May. An agreement in the engineering industry entails an hourly wage increase of NKr 1 with effect from April.

May

The Revised 1994 Budget is presented to Parliament:
- the State budget deficit is expected to reach NKr 42½ billion in 1994, broadly in line with the initial projections;
- excluding oil and gas revenue, the budget deficit is expected to be about NKr 65½ billion;
- the Budget reiterates the central bank's commitment to maintain a stable exchange rate against European currencies within the fluctuation range that has prevailed since the krone was floated on 10 December 1992.

Den norske Bank initiates a private placement of 54 million shares of NKr 16.75 each, raising the bank's share capital by NKr 888 million.

The EU approves the "oil directive" regulating the exploration of oil and gas in the EEA.

June

Parliament decides to convert the public corporation Norwegian Telecom into a state-owned limited company.

Amendments in Parliament on the Revised 1994 Budget entail that:
- the reduced VAT tariff on certain food products will be maintained;
- the excise duty on cigarettes and electricity tax will be raised;

– the lending rate of the State Educational Loan Fund will be reduced from 8½ to 7 per cent (excluding loans issued more than seven years ago).

Norway signs the Accession Treaty with the EU on Corfu on 24 June.

July

Increases in excise duties on petrol, diesel, tobacco and motor vehicles and the rise in the electricity tax take effect on 1 July.

September

The government presents proposals changing the conditions for petroleum activities on the Norwegian Continental Shelf (NCS), including reduced government participation in acreage allocated in the 15th licensing round and a review of State shares in licenses already awarded.

October

The government presents the draft National Budget for 1995. Based upon an oil price assumption of NKr 115 per barrel, the State budget deficit for 1995 is projected at NKr 20.9 billion; excluding oil-related revenues and expenditures the deficit is expected to reach NKr 52.6 billion.

The Russian Foreign Minister approves an earlier agreement between the government of Azarbaijan and Statoil/British Petroleum to produce oil in the Caspian Sea.

The Working Environment Bill, presented by the Parliamentary Standing Committee on Local Government and Environment, stipulates a ban on temporary employment contracts for companies' regular activities.

Statoil reports a large gas discovery in the North Sea close to the Gullfaks field, containing 60 billion cubic metres.

Parliament endorses an increase in income taxation related to the imputed return of owner-occupied housing. Henceforth the rate of return is fixed at 2½ per cent for houses with an assessed value of up to NKr 440 000, and at 5 per cent for more expensive houses. In both cases the first NKr 50 000 are tax free.

November

The General Auditor refuses to approve the accounts of the Postal Giro on the grounds that unexplained discrepancies and accounting errors have been discovered.

In a referendum on Norwegian membership to the EU, a majority of 52.2 per cent of the electorate vote No and 47.8 vote Yes.

December

Statoil announces the conclusion of contracts for steel deliveries by European and Japanese suppliers for five new gas pipeline projects – at NKr 8 billion the largest ever on the NCS.

The government presents the final National Budget Bill for 1995, proposing a 1 percentage point increase in the value-added tax in order to achieve a larger reduction in the budget deficit than initially proposed.

Under the auspices of the OECD, representatives of the Nordic countries, the EU, the United States, Japan and South Korea sign an agreement prohibiting all State support to shipbuilding.

1995

January

The EFTA's surveillance body ESA declares the retail monopoly for wine and spirits in Norway as a violation of the EEA Agreement's prohibition of quantitative trade restrictions and provision on monopolies.

The Gas Negotiation Committee signs an agreement with Total and Gaz de France concerning the sale of natural gas to France. The agreement covers deliveries of 40 million tons of oil equivalents in 26 years, starting in 2001.

Parliament rejects government proposals on a change in the so-called split model for income taxation of self employed.

February

The Ministry of Industry and Energy announces 56 blocks on the NCS to be open for exploration in the framework of the 15th licensing round.

The government decides to abolish the State import monopoly for wine and spirits, although it would maintain the retail monopoly of these products.

March

The government endorses the EU's licensing directive for oil activities, implying that oil and gas are henceforth included under the provisions of the EEA Agreement.

May

The Revised 1995 Budget is presented to Parliament. Based upon an assumed oil price of NKr 115 per barrel, the State budget deficit is expected to reach NKr 6 billion in 1995, compared with a projected NKr 11 billion in the December Budget Bill.

STATISTICAL ANNEX AND STRUCTURAL INDICATORS

Table A. **Selected background statistics**

	Average 1985-94	1985	1986	1987	1988	1989	1990	1991	1992	1993	1994
A. Percentage changes											
Private consumption[1]	2.0	9.9	5.6	-1.0	-2.8	-2.8	2.8	0	1.8	2.3	4.4
Government consumption[1]	2.6	3.3	2.2	4.0	0.5	2.6	2.1	2.6	4.4	1.8	2.7
Gross fixed capital formation[1]	-0.6	-13.9	23.9	-2.1	1.6	-3.9	-26.8	1.7	4.5	13.9	4.8
Residential[1]	-4.5	4.1	9.6	4.0	-3.8	-17.0	-17.1	-27.3	-12.6	-5.2	33.7
Oil sector[1]	2.5	-42.9	62.4	-18.5	-4.2	25.0	-62.7	88.4	31.3	50.3	2.0
Ships and pipelines[1]	-4.8	-256.0	67.8	-61.9	-448.9	48.3	-62.0	-45.0	-111.5	-593.5	0
Other private business sector[1]	-2.5	11.5	21.2	-6.0	-17.6	-24.4	2.6	-10.3	3.7	-3.3	5.8
Public[1]	2.3	-3.6	15.0	10.0	7.4	0.7	-7.1	14.4	5.3	-10.4	-4.8
Total domestic demand[1]	1.1	3.2	7.9	-1.3	-3.0	-2.9	-0.9	-0.5	1.7	3.0	4.8
Exports of goods and services[1]	5.5	6.9	1.6	1.2	5.5	10.7	8.1	6.1	6.2	1.6	7.6
Imports of goods and services[1]	2.4	5.9	9.9	-7.3	-1.7	0.9	2.2	1.7	2.8	3.2	7.2
GDP[1]	2.5	5.3	4.2	2.0	-0.5	0.6	1.7	1.6	3.4	2.3	5.1
Mainland GDP[1]	1.5	5.9	3.4	1.2	-1.7	-2.2	1.1	-0.6	2.1	2.0	3.9
GDP price deflator	2.9	5.0	-1.4	7.2	4.4	5.9	4.5	2.4	-1.0	2.0	0.3
Industrial production	2.0	11.0	1.1	1.0	-1.2	0.2	0.1	-1.6	1.2	2.1	6.6
Manufacturing	1.7	7.6	1.1	0.9	-1.2	0.3	-0.1	-1.0	1.5	2.0	6.7
Employment	0.3	2.3	3.5	1.9	-0.6	-3.0	-1.0	-1.0	-0.3	0	1.5
Compensation of employees (current prices)	6.1	10.8	13.2	12.9	5.9	1.3	4.1	4.2	3.4	1.2	4.9
Productivity (real GDP/employment)	2.2	2.9	0.6	0.1	0.1	3.7	2.6	2.6	3.6	2.3	3.5
Unit labour costs (compensation/real GDP)	3.5	5.2	8.7	10.7	6.4	0.7	2.4	2.6	0	-1.1	-0.2
B. Percentage ratios											
Gross fixed capital formation as per cent of GDP at constant prices	23.0	23.4	27.9	26.8	27.3	26.1	18.8	18.8	19.0	21.1	21.1
Stockbuilding as per cent of GDP at constant prices	-0.3	2.5	1.3	0.3	-1.8	-2.7	1.7	0.3	-0.8	-2.2	-1.5
Foreign balance as per cent of GDP at constant prices	4.9	-1.5	-4.6	-1.2	1.5	5.1	7.6	9.5	11.0	10.4	10.7
Compensation of employees as per cent of GDP at current prices	52.1	47.9	52.8	54.5	55.5	52.8	51.7	51.9	52.4	50.8	50.5
Direct taxes as per cent of household income	16.5	15.1	15.2	16.1	17.5	17.7	17.3	17.0	15.9	16.6	16.6
Household saving as per cent of disposable income	0.1	-2.7	-6.1	-6.2	-2.4	0.9	0.9	2.6	5.2	4.5	4.4
Unemployment rate	4.3	2.6	2.0	2.1	3.2	4.9	5.2	5.5	5.9	6.0	5.5
C. Other indicator											
Current balance (billion dollars)	0.8	3.1	-4.5	-4.1	-3.9	0.2	3.9	5.1	2.9	2.2	3.6
Excluding shipping and oil platforms	2.7	-3.6	-11.9	-8.9	5.0	19.6	10.6	2.9	-3.7	9.5	7.2

1. At constant prices.
Source: Central Bureau of Statistics; OECD estimates.

Table B. Supply and use of resources

Kr million, current prices

	1985	1986	1987	1988	1989	1990	1991	1992	1993	1994
Private consumption	245 439	278 909	298 053	307 498	311 954	336 064	349 703	365 151	380 464	402 662
Government consumption	92 654	101 580	116 045	122 238	130 998	139 116	147 478	157 220	161 779	169 527
Gross fixed investment	110 043	145 540	157 363	170 345	169 486	124 145	127 053	135 245	161 153	141 798
Stockbuilding	11 101	6 070	1 221	-12 519	-18 328	11 053	2 019	-5 782	-18 246	11 169
Total domestic demand	459 237	532 099	572 682	587 562	594 110	610 378	626 253	651 834	685 150	725 156
Exports	235 564	194 662	200 224	213 671	261 863	293 014	307 527	303 155	316 825	335 672
Imports	194 602	213 044	211 427	217 957	234 592	242 846	247 098	252 037	267 487	286 584
GDP at market prices	500 199	513 717	561 479	583 276	621 381	660 546	686 682	702 952	734 488	774 244
Indirect taxes	91 037	99 922	107 493	106 984	106 562	111 089	115 617	121 441	128 733	..
Subsidies	26 936	29 569	31 515	33 769	36 599	39 992	42 826	44 396	49 146	..
GDP at factor costs	436 098	443 364	485 501	510 061	551 418	589 449	613 891	625 907	654 901	..
Depreciation and other operating provisions	66 511	72 560	83 300	91 193	96 677	98 819	102 514	104 189	110 227	..
Net domestic product at factor costs	369 587	370 804	402 201	418 868	454 741	490 630	511 377	521 718	544 674	..

Source: Norwegian National Accounts.

Table C. Gross domestic product by origin

Kr million, current prices

	1985	1986	1987	1988	1989	1990	1991	1992	1993	1994
Agriculture, forestry and fishing	15 150	16 021	17 695	17 689	17 568	20 330	20 052	..	..	..
Crude petroleum and natural gas production	89 706	50 966	51 759	44 383	69 755	86 912	89 670	..	..	..
Pipeline transport	2 987	5 663	5 987	5 966	7 136	7 962	9 994	..	..	..
Mining and quarrying	1 303	1 564	1 639	1 568	1 865	1 733	1 702	..	..	..
Manufacturing	70 127	75 651	84 590	89 506	91 265	90 368	92 591	..	..	..
Electricity supply	17 797	19 077	20 892	22 912	24 326	25 908	26 386	..	..	..
Construction	23 221	27 831	34 334	36 349	30 651	27 625	24 705	..	..	..
Wholesale and retail trade	47 298	54 694	58 893	61 197	61 426	64 934	66 663	..	..	..
Hotels and restaurants	6 598	7 871	9 225	9 033	8 558	8 284	8 652	..	..	..
Ocean transport and drilling	13 753	11 617	8 547	11 242	16 322	18 146	23 250	..	..	..
Other transports and communications	25 084	28 971	32 188	36 150	38 109	40 254	40 693	..	..	..
Financing and insurance	16 625	22 792	27 876	27 766	28 908	28 029	27 898	..	..	..
Business services	21 652	25 054	28 332	30 809	30 768	30 933	32 321	..	..	..
Dwelling services	18 105	19 711	21 796	25 367	28 940	32 287	33 811	..	..	..
Other private services	21 889	25 322	27 936	30 091	30 332	32 844	34 910	..	..	..
Producers of government services	67 965	75 370	85 629	91 930	97 841	104 125	111 910	..	..	..
Correction items	40 941	45 544	44 166	41 321	37 614	39 875	41 478	..	..	..
GDP at market prices	500 203	513 721	561 482	583 279	621 385	660 550	686 685	..	..	..

Source: Norwegian National Accounts.

Table D. **Gross domestic product by origin**
Volume, 1985 = 100

	1985	1986	1987	1988	1989	1990	1991	1992	1993	1994
Agriculture, forestry and fishing	100.0	94.1	98.5	99.6	102.5	114.2	115.3	114.2	123.3	124.7
Crude petroleum and natural gas production	100.0	106.4	120.5	135.2	171.3	176.4	201.3	226.6	240.1	270.2
Pipeline transport	100.0	169.2	190.5	185.5	220.3	217.6	239.2	266.4	282.2	316.5
Mining and quarrying	100.0	120.0	120.2	105.4	117.1	114.5	109.3	110.6	110.0	115.4
Manufacturing	100.0	100.0	101.9	97.0	95.4	96.1	94.0	95.7	97.3	102.2
Electricity gas and water supply	100.0	92.7	98.7	105.1	115.7	116.2	104.8	111.1	113.3	106.9
Construction	100.0	109.8	113.8	112.7	103.7	99.5	94.0	94.0	91.1	94.9
Wholesale and retail trade	100.0	105.9	103.8	98.2	96.2	96.7	95.6	96.7	99.0	105.4
Hotels and restaurants	100.0	107.5	111.3	101.9	90.2	83.8	85.6	86.1	89.1	95.9
Ocean transport and drilling	100.0	97.4	77.0	73.9	88.1	102.4	106.3	102.5	95.3	93.0
Other transports and communications	100.0	109.0	112.7	120.5	120.6	127.9	133.7	132.8	135.0	147.3
Financing and insurance	100.0	104.7	111.7	115.1	106.6	102.4	95.9	93.9	94.3	95.7
Business services	100.0	104.3	108.7	108.2	103.0	96.1	95.0	96.9	99.0	102.3
Dwelling services	100.0	103.2	108.4	114.9	121.3	124.8	123.3	123.9	124.3	124.9
Other private services	100.0	107.3	107.7	108.7	104.9	107.7	108.7	112.0	113.7	116.9
Producers of government services	100.0	101.7	104.6	106.9	108.7	111.5	115.2	119.3	122.6	125.2
Correction items	100.0	105.8	93.7	76.7	64.6	66.9	67.1	71.3	74.3	81.3
GDP at market prices	100.0	104.2	106.3	105.7	106.4	108.1	109.8	113.5	116.3	122.3

Source: Norwegian National Accounts.

Table E. **General government income and expenditure**

Kr million

	1985	1986	1987	1988	1989	1990	1991	1992	1993	1994
Current receipts	275 435	281 097	309 816	321 356	341 444	371 880	379 324	387 126	403 038	428 146
Indirect taxes	91 037	99 922	107 493	106 984	106 562	111 089	115 617	121 441	128 733	139 392
Social security contributions	57 304	67 460	79 718	79 632	76 604	80 239	83 698	87 917	84 383	89 024
Direct taxes	100 600	79 309	87 951	96 505	107 395	118 449	120 050	119 838	127 400	136 697
Capital income	23 053	30 855	33 463	32 942	42 673	51 099	53 060	51 525	55 559	51 605
Other current receipts	3 441	3 551	1 191	5 293	8 210	11 004	6 899	6 405	6 963	11 428
Current expenditure	215 012	239 946	268 976	290 330	316 702	341 280	363 642	386 012	403 311	416 419
Expenditure on goods and services	92 654	101 580	116 045	122 238	130 998	139 116	147 478	157 220	161 792	169 771
Subsidies	26 936	29 569	31 515	33 769	36 599	39 992	42 826	44 396	49 146	51 260
Interest paid	17 393	22 325	24 061	22 670	24 705	25 805	24 836	25 648	27 800	27 501
Current transfers	4 210	4 947	5 283	6 295	6 249	7 385	7 631	8 076	7 763	8 466
Net saving	60 423	41 151	40 840	31 026	24 742	30 600	15 682	1 114	−273	11 727
Consumption of fixed capital	3 742	4 259	4 845	5 355	5 678	5 933	6 220	6 584	6 767	7 553
Gross saving	64 165	45 410	45 685	36 381	30 420	36 533	21 902	7 698	6 494	19 280
Gross fixed capital formation	13 288	16 458	20 087	22 650	23 020	21 423	24 307	25 625	22 748	22 180
Net lending	51 189	29 932	26 440	15 269	8 926	16 476	−1 505	−16 456	−15 648	−1 846
Memorandum item:										
Revenue from oil sector	50 598	18 268	15 402	9 940	24 573	40 684	46 269	38 248	44 569	43 628

Source: Norwegian National Accounts; OECD, *National Accounts.*

116

Table F. Labour market
Thousand persons

	1985	1986	1987	1988	1989	1990	1991	1992	1993	1994
Civilian employment	1 984	2 053	2 090	2 079	2 014	1 992	1 973	1 970	1 970	..
Agriculture, forestry and fishing	147	151	139	134	132	129	116	110	111	..
Oil production and mining	22	22	24	24	23	22	21	25	25	..
Manufacturing	348	358	352	337	318	310	294	295	292	..
Electricity, gas and water	19	21	23	21	22	23	21	20	22	..
Construction	151	155	166	166	147	139	130	122	116	..
Wholesale and retail trade	346	364	375	376	369	358	354	353	349	..
Transports and communications	175	179	178	175	167	162	162	157	158	..
Banking insurance real estate	128	142	155	166	154	150	153	153	153	..
Community, social and personal services	644	658	673	674	675	696	716	729	741	..
Registered unemployment	51.4	36.2	32.4	49.3	82.9	92.7	100.7	114.4	118.2	110.3
Unfilled vacancies	5.8	10.5	12.4	8.7	6.9	6.6	6.5	6.4	7.4	7.7
Unemployment rate (per cent of labour force)	2.6	2.0	2.1	3.2	4.9	5.2	5.5	5.9	6.0	5.4

Source: OECD, Labour Force Statistics, Main Economic Indicators.

Table G. Balance of payments

Million US dollars

	1985	1986	1987	1988	1989	1990	1991	1992	1993	1994
Current account										
Merchandise exports	19 937	18 158	21 179	23 053	27 174	34 072	34 095	35 166	31 968	34 804
Crude petroleum and natural gas	11 260	7 173	8 603	7 434	11 117	14 988	16 190	14 031	13 843	15 870
Ships and oil platforms	1 505	1 550	1 626	872	975	1 780	2 357	1 899	1 450	1 155
Other	7 172	9 435	10 950	14 747	15 082	17 304	15 547	19 235	16 675	17 779
Merchandise imports	15 199	20 250	21 899	23 239	23 392	26 475	25 439	25 853	24 025	26 523
Ships and oil platforms	693	625	978	2 310	3 919	3 051	2 334	1 004	1 674	1 406
Other	14 506	19 625	20 921	20 929	19 473	23 424	23 105	24 849	22 351	25 117
Trade balance	4 738	-2 092	-720	-186	3 782	7 598	8 656	9 313	7 943	8 281
Services, net	-1 078	-1 625	-2 360	-2 552	-2 416	-2 326	-2 068	-4 632	-2 826	-1 077
Travel	-1 067	-1 556	-1 853	-2 056	-1 642	-2 097	-1 770	-2 057	-1 838	-1 896
Investment income	-1 034	-1 129	-1 242	-1 955	-2 515	-2 676	-2 607	-3 433	-3 247	-1 718
Other services	1 023	1 060	735	1 459	1 741	2 447	2 309	858	2 259	2 537
Transfers, net	-555	-808	-978	-1 134	-1 127	-1 417	-1 514	-1 791	-1 399	-1 622
Private	-65	-140	-194	-168	-222	-237	-338	-491	-304	-448
Official	-490	-668	-784	-966	-905	-1 180	-1 176	-1 300	-1 095	-1 174
Current balance	3 105	-4 524	-4 058	-3 872	239	3 855	5 075	2 889	3 719	5 582
Capital account										
Long-term capital net	-1 030	2 817	19	4 599	3 028	-1 322	-2 885	2 540	1 188	-2 394
Private, direct	-1 640	-582	-706	-683	159	-474	-2 131	286	1 069	-985
Private, portfolio	1 744	4 286	2 346	4 185	3 060	514	-2 966	949	-404	87
Private, other	-1 045	-734	-1 558	1 230	-188	-1 568	2 009	1 231	584	-1 317
Public[1]	-89	-152	-63	-132	-2	207	203	75	-61	-178
Short-term capital, net	2 582	116	5 501	107	-1 035	642	-4 604	-3 471	6 058	-228
Private non monetary	182	1 287	317	155	-659	361	726	3 188	1 576	801
Private monetary institutions	2 400	-1 171	5 184	-48	-376	281	-5 330	-6 659	4 482	-1 029
Miscellaneous official accounts	-1	25	-25	65	-58	-37	40	711	-4 146	1 476
Errors and omissions	-1 199	-1 650	-1 258	-1 063	-1 355	-2 803	-417	-3 372	-1 290	-758
Change in reserves	3 447	-3 169	-84	-225	903	357	-2 767	-728	3 957	1 559

1. Excludes special transactions.
Source: OECD.

118

Table H. Foreign trade by area

Million US dollars

	1984	1985	1986	1987	1988	1989	1990	1991	1992	1993
Imports total	13 885	15 554	20 298	22 578	23 211	23 668	27 200	25 523	26 064	24 003
OECD countries	12 268	13 935	18 521	20 220	19 275	18 222	22 385	21 528	22 764	20 928
EEC	6 549	7 643	10 163	11 196	10 638	10 085	12 335	12 211	12 607	11 609
of which:										
Germany	2 007	2 500	3 436	3 495	3 145	2 972	3 768	3 608	3 758	3 250
Belgium-Luxembourg	384	433	596	650	585	618	634	612	623	584
France	636	650	824	832	767	770	1 009	975	1 058	1 024
Netherlands	478	550	775	868	906	781	1 068	1 341	1 027	984
United Kingdom	1 426	1 553	1 783	2 020	1 724	1 681	2 325	2 128	2 315	2 126
USA	1 243	1 118	1 393	1 452	1 527	1 724	2 388	1 986	2 224	1 932
Sweden	2 383	2 776	3 644	4 265	4 071	3 586	4 234	3 927	4 011	3 378
Finland	673	632	811	981	808	711	843	804	921	786
Non-OECD countries	1 616	1 619	1 768	2 347	3 792	5 290	4 687	3 880	3 176	2 964
COMECON	502	434	366	445	528	593	685	544	635	613
OPEC	102	128	82	65	112	117	144	127	70	63
Others	1 013	1 058	1 320	1 837	3 152	4 580	3 858	3 208	2 471	2 289
Exports total	18 914	19 934	18 230	21 449	22 429	27 101	34 033	34 037	35 138	31 893
OECD countries	17 186	17 682	15 689	18 875	20 073	24 536	30 643	30 424	31 196	28 200
EEC	13 377	13 846	11 859	13 803	14 343	17 324	21 653	22 262	23 034	20 865
of which:										
Germany	3 120	3 104	3 485	3 193	2 699	2 934	3 680	3 703	4 548	4 077
Belgium-Luxembourg	170	193	215	288	557	672	723	821	1 003	721
France	642	1 048	627	1 086	1 596	2 380	2 606	2 537	2 686	2 459
Netherlands	1 379	1 214	1 086	1 562	1 497	1 753	2 636	2 668	2 480	2 686
United Kingdom	6 892	7 103	5 060	5 711	5 786	7 221	8 853	8 937	8 454	7 736
USA	964	1 021	988	1 222	1 334	1 775	2 168	1 609	1 825	1 934
Sweden	1 865	1 752	1 805	2 387	2 564	3 238	3 834	3 447	3 209	2 692
Finland	276	315	317	421	468	558	916	1 014	877	795
Non-OECD countries	1 728	2 251	2 541	2 574	1 715	1 796	2 622	2 971	3 230	2 899
COMECON	164	175	174	223	270	287	382	406	488	497
OPEC	102	100	122	112	100	94	413	116	166	149
Others	1 462	1 977	2 246	2 240	1 345	1 415	1 826	2 449	2 576	2 252

Source: OECD, *Foreign Trade Statistics, Series C.*

Table I. **Prices and wages**

1990 = 100

	1985	1986	1987	1988	1989	1990	1991	1992	1993	1994
Consumer prices										
Total	73.9	79.2	86.1	91.9	96.0	100.0	103.4	105.8	108.2	109.8
Food	75.5	82.4	88.6	94.3	96.9	100.0	101.7	103.1	102.1	103.5
Rent heating and light	72.6	76.2	81.9	88.6	94.0	100.0	104.5	107.0	110.0	111.0
Wholesale prices										
Total	79.7	81.9	86.8	91.4	96.5	100.0	102.5	102.6	102.5	104.0
Consumer goods	76.9	81.4	86.9	91.9	95.7	100.0	103.7	105.6	105.7	107.1
Investment goods	79.7	85.1	90.5	94.6	97.9	100.0	102.1	103.0	106.2	108.2
Petroleum products	110.8	77.1	81.2	72.7	84.4	100.0	100.2	91.4	93.2	91.0
Hourly earnings										
Males	66.8	73.6	85.6	90.2	94.5	100.0	105.1	108.5	111.4	114.6
Females	64.6	71.4	82.9	88.1	93.5	100.0	106.0	109.1	112.3	115.6

Source: OECD, *Main Economic Indicators*; Secretariat estimates.

Table J. **Money and credit**

Kr million

	1985	1986	1987	1988	1989	1990	1991	1992	1993	1994
Changes in money supply										
Central authorities[1]	10 566	-3 696	16 784	16 568	34 836	46 465	60 308	82 400	37 500	39 000
Commercial and saving banks[2]	63 677	50 651	83 298	11 290	1 303	1 076	12 520	-33 400	-26 300	20 900
Unspecified and statistical errors	-940	14 695	-9 739	-6 200	-17 396	-17 498	-8 811	-9 200	-9 500	-13 400
Domestic liquidity supply	73 303	61 650	90 343	21 658	18 743	30 043	64 017	39 800	1 700	46 500
Foreign transactions	-31 572	-47 176	-40 252	300	11 794	-4 147	-15 101	-2 400	1 300	-10 400
Change in broad money (M2)	41 731	14 474	50 091	21 958	30 537	25 896	48 916	37 400	3 000	36 100
Domestic lending										
by financial institutions										
Total[3]	470 984	571 850	692 160	765 431	823 750	843 424	823 842	808 863	796 696	808 785
Commercial banks	132 679	173 610	211 822	222 678	247 639	250 987	231 892	235 584	228 693	235 156
Saving banks	104 056	129 822	159 072	173 158	184 100	191 950	191 652	192 312	202 474	216 855
State banks	121 793	129 559	137 446	145 777	154 725	163 044	174 949	185 586	180 794	176 693
Insurance companies	36 971	46 809	55 597	59 414	59 313	61 199	70 091	78 302	70 888	66 610
Mortgage credit institutions	52 774	67 467	99 870	126 488	142 782	144 659	121 606	83 132	73 144	63 219
Private finance institutions	17 355	18 751	21 898	30 347	25 963	20 742	19 986	17 636	18 981	24 016
Postal saving banks	4 993	5 460	6 047	7 101	8 394	10 196	13 089	15 246	20 873	25 623

1. Government income surplus loan transactions, Central and State banks. Excluding oil taxes.
2. Including tax-free allocations to funds and saving with tax productions.
3. Breakdown does not add up to total.
Source: Bank of Norway, Economic Bulletin; Central Bureau of Statistics, Monthly Bulletin of Statistics.

Table K. Production and employment structures

	Per cent share of GDP at factor cost (current prices)				Per cent share of total employment			
	1962	1970	1980	1991	1962	1970	1980	1991
Agriculture, forestry and fishing	7.9	5.6	3.8	2.9	19.0	12.9	8.4	6.1
Mining, crude petroleum and natural gas	0.8	0.7	14.8	13.3	0.6	0.6	0.8	1.1
Manufacturing	21.1	21.6	16.0	13.5	23.4	23.8	19.8	14.3
of which:								
Food, forestry and tobacco	3.9	3.3	1.7	3.0	3.7	3.6	3.1	2.5
Textiles, clothing, leather	2.3	1.5	0.7	0.3	3.2	2.4	1.2	0.5
Wood and wood products	1.6	1.8	1.4	0.8	2.1	2.2	1.9	1.2
Paper and paper products	2.6	2.8	2.0	2.1	3.4	3.5	2.8	2.4
Chemicals and products of petroleum, coal, rubber, etc.	2.1	2.3	1.9	1.6	3.0	3.0	2.5	1.9
Fabricated metal products, machinery and equipment	5.7	6.4	5.6	4.3	6.4	7.4	6.8	4.9
Electricity, gas and water	2.8	2.7	2.9	4.0	0.9	0.9	0.9	1.0
Construction	8.0	7.0	5.9	3.9	8.1	8.2	7.9	6.9
Services	59.4	62.4	56.5	62.4	48.2	53.7	62.3	70.6
of which:								
Wholesale and retail trade, restaurants and hotels	20.1	12.4	11.7	11.0	14.4	15.5	16.6	16.5
Transport, storage and communication	14.7	14.7	9.4	10.4	11.2	10.2	9.1	8.9
Finance, insurance, real estate and business services	9.5	9.1	9.9	13.7	2.7	3.7	5.0	7.3
Producers of Government services	9.7	11.8	13.6	16.3	12.8	16.6	23.2	28.7

Source: OECD, National Accounts.

122

Table L. **Productivity and investment structure**

	Productivity growth (sector GDP/sector employment)				Investment per cent of total investment[1]			
	1963-69	1970-79	1980-91	1991	1962	1970	1980	1991
Agriculture, forestry and fishing	4.4	3.3	4.6	5.6	8.0	6.6	8.2	3.8
Mining, crude petroleum and natural gas	8.7	25.7	6.5	9.5	0.6	2.4	9.7	20.5
Manufacturing	4.6	1.7	2.3	1.4	17.1	15.3	12.8	10.3
of which:								
Food, forestry and tobacco	3.8	0.2	-0.1	4.5	3.2	2.9	2.3	2.0
Textiles, clothing, leather	3.1	0.6	4.2	8.0	0.7	0.5	0.4	0.1
Wood and wood products	6.4	1.6	0.5	-0.1	0.5	1.2	0.8	0.6
Paper and paper products	5.2	-0.1	2.0	0.4	2.8	1.8	3.0	1.7
Chemicals and products of petroleum, coal, rubber, etc.	8.1	4.0	4.8	-8.1	3.3	2.0	1.4	2.0
Fabricated metal products, machinery and equipment	2.9	1.3	2.4	3.5	3.4	3.4	2.6	2.1
Electricity, gas and water	5.2	0.7	0.7	-8.3	10.4	8.1	9.9	5.1
Construction	2.8	2.5	0.2	3.3	1.3	2.0	2.2	1.8
Services	2.4	1.7	0.5	0.2	62.6	65.5	57.3	58.5
of which:								
Wholesale and retail trade, restaurants and hotels	1.3	-0.6	-0.2	1.7	4.7	4.6	4.6	4.2
Transport, storage and communication	4.5	3.3	3.7	5.1	25.8	20.5	10.9	16.7
Finance, insurance, real estate and business services	-0.2	-1.6	-1.8	-0.9	19.2	21.8	23.9	16.6
Producers of Government services	2.0	0.5	0.8	0.3	12.1	16.9	16.2	19.1

1. At current prices.
Source: OECD, *National Accounts.*

123

Table M. **Labour market indicators**

A. LABOUR MARKET PERFORMANCE

	Cyclical trough: 1983	Cyclical peak: 1986	1988	1993
Standardised unemployment rate	3.4	2.0	3.2	6.0
Unemployment rate: Total	3.4	2.0	3.1	6.0
Male	3.2	1.6	3.0	6.6
Women	3.8	2.4	3.3	5.2
Youth [1]	8.9	5.0	7.9	13.9
Share of long-term unemployment in total unemployment [2]	5.8	7.1	5.8	..

B. STRUCTURAL OR INSTITUTIONAL CHARACTERISTICS

	1975	1980	1985	1993
Participation rate: [3] Total	69.8	76.7	80.0	77.8
Male	85.5	88.7	89.7	83.4
Women	53.6	64.2	70.1	71.9
Employment/population (15-64 years)	69.1	74.0	75.5	72.8
Non-wage labour costs [4] (as a percentage of total compensation)	14.9	14.6	14.3	13.4
Unemployment insurance replacement ratio [5]	7.2	23.6	34.9	44.2

	Average percentage changes(annual rates)			
	1970 / 1960	1980 / 1970	1990 / 1980	1993 / 1991
Labour force	0.7	2.2	1.3	0
Employment: Total	0.7	2.1	1.2	0
Industries	1.2	0	–0.7	–1.5
Services	2.0	4.7	2.4	0.4

1. People between 16 and 24 years as a percentage of the labour force of the same age group.
2. Persons seeking a job for 12 months and over as a percentage of total unemployed.
3. Labour force as a percentage of relevant population group aged between 15 and 64 years.
4. Employers' contributions to social security and pension funds.
5. Unemployment benefits per unemployed as a percentage of compensation per employee.
Source: OECD, *Labour Force Statistics*; OECD.

Table N. Public sector
General government income and expenditure structures

As a percentage of GDP

	1962	1970	1980	1993
Current receipts	35.5	43.5	53.2	54.9
Indirect taxes	14.1	18.2	17.2	17.5
Social security contributions	6.3	9.7	12.0	11.5
Direct taxes	13.4	13.3	21.5	17.4
Capital income	1.7	2.3	2.5	7.6
Other current receipts	0	0	0.1	0.9
Current expenditure	28.0	36.5	44.3	54.9
Expenditure on goods and services	14.0	16.9	18.8	22.0
Defence	3.4	3.5	2.8	..
Education	3.7	4.9	5.1	..
Health	1.5	2.4	4.1	..
Social security and welfare	0.8	0.9	1.6	..
Economic services	2.2	2.4	2.3	..
Other	2.5	2.8	2.9	..
Subsidies	4.2	5.2	7.0	6.7
Interest paid	1.5	1.8	3.4	3.8
Current transfers	8.4	12.6	15.1	22.4
Net saving	7.6	7.0	8.9	0
Consumption of fixed capital	0.6	0.7	0.8	0.9
Gross saving	8.1	7.7	9.7	0.9
Gross fixed capital formation	3.5	4.5	4.0	3.1
Net lending	4.6	3.2	5.7	–2.1
Memorandum item:				
Revenue from oil sector	0	0	8.2	3.6

Source: Norwegian National Accounts; OECD, *National Accounts.*

BASIC STATISTICS

BASIC STATISTICS:

INTERNATIONAL COMPARISONS

	Units	Reference period [1]	Australia	Austria
Population				
Total	Thousands	1992	17 489	7 884
Inhabitants per sq. km	Number	1992	2	94
Net average annual increase over previous 10 years	%	1992	1.4	0.4
Employment				
Civilian employment (CE)[2]	Thousands	1992	7 637	3 546
Of which: Agriculture	% of CE		5.3	7.1
Industry	% of CE		23.8	35.6
Services	% of CE		71	57.4
Gross domestic product (GDP)				
At current prices and current exchange rates	Bill. US$	1992	296.6	186.2
Per capita	US$		16 959	23 616
At current prices using current PPPs[3]	Bill. US$	1992	294.5	142
Per capita	US$		16 800	18 017
Average annual volume growth over previous 5 years	%	1992	2	3.4
Gross fixed capital formation (GFCF)	% of GDP	1992	19.7	25
Of which: Machinery and equipment	% of GDP		9.3	9.9
Residential construction	% of GDP		5.1	5.7
Average annual volume growth over previous 5 years	%	1992	−1	5.1
Gross saving ratio[4]	% of GDP	1992	15.6	25.1
General government				
Current expenditure on goods and services	% of GDP	1992	18.5	18.4
Current disbursements[5]	% of GDP	1992	36.9	46.2
Current receipts	% of GDP	1992	33.1	48.3
Net official development assistance	% of GNP	1992	0.33	0.3
Indicators of living standards				
Private consumption per capita using current PPPs[3]	US$	1992	10 527	9 951
Passenger cars, per 1 000 inhabitants	Number	1990	430	382
Telephones, per 1 000 inhabitants	Number	1990	448	589
Television sets, per 1 000 inhabitants	Number	1989	484	475
Doctors, per 1 000 inhabitants	Number	1991	2	2.1
Infant mortality per 1 000 live births	Number	1991	7.1	7.4
Wages and prices (average annual increase over previous 5 years)				
Wages (earnings or rates according to availability)	%	1992	5	5.4
Consumer prices	%	1992	5.2	3
Foreign trade				
Exports of goods, fob*	Mill. US$	1992	42 844	44 361
As % of GDP	%		14.4	23.8
Average annual increase over previous 5 years	%		10.1	10.4
Imports of goods, cif*	Mill. US$	1992	40 751	54 038
As % of GDP	%		13.7	29
Average annual increase over previous 5 years	%		8.6	10.7
Total official reserves[6]	Mill. SDRs	1992	8 152	9 006
As ratio of average monthly imports of goods	Ratio		2.4	2

* At current prices and exchange rates.
1. Unless otherwise stated.
2. According to the definitions used in OECD *Labour Force Statistics.*
3. PPPs = Purchasing Power Parities.
4. Gross saving = Gross national disposable income minus private and government consumption.
5. Current disbursements = Current expenditure on goods and services plus current transfers and payments of property income.
6. Gold included in reserves is valued at 35 SDRs per ounce. End of year.
7. Including Luxembourg.

gium	Can.al	Spain	Sweden	Switzerland	Turkey	United Kingdom	United States
045	28 58	39 085	8 668	6 875	58 400	57 998	255 610
329	)7	77	19	166	75	237	27
0.2	0	0.3	0.4	0.6	2.2	0.3	1
724	12)8	12 359	4 195	3 481	18 600	25 175	117 598
2.6	.6	10.1	3.3	5.6	43.9	2.2	2.9
27.7	2.2	32.4	26.5	33.9	22.1	26.5	24.6
69.7	.3	57.5	70.2	60.6	34	71.3	72.5
220.9	56.2	576.3	247.2	240.9	159.1	1 042.8	5 937.3
991	19 ₁1	14 745	28 522	35 041	2 724	17 981	23 228
181.5	53.9	500.2	143.3	152.8	297.3	941.1	5 953.3
071	19 ₁3	12 797	16 526	22 221	5 019	16 227	23 291
3.1	.3	3.3	0.6	1.7	3.7	0.9	1.9
19.1	1.2	21.8	17	23.7	23	15.6	15.6
8.6	..	6.8	6.2	8	8.5	7.2	7.2
4.6	..	4.3	5.9	15.7 [10]	7.6	3	3.7
7.1	.8	6.2	−0.6	1.5	4.6	0.6	0.7
21.3	1.3	19.1	14.1	29.7	23.1	12.8	14.5
14.7	2.3	17	27.8	14.3	12.9	22.3	17.7
54.6	4 ..	..	64.6	35.1	..	42.1	36.7
49.7	4 ..	..	59.6	34.7	..	38	31.6
0.39	0.6	0.26	1	0.47	..	0.31	0.2
420	11 ₁4	8 083	8 907	13 043	3 206	10 397	15 637
387	₅0	307	418	441	29	361	568
546	₅3	323	681	905	151	434	509
447	₆6	389	471	406	174	434	814
3.6	.8	3.9	2.9	3	0.9	1.4	2.3
8.4	.8	7.8	6.1	6.2	56.5	7.4	8.9
4.1	..	7.7	7.3	..	..	8.3	2.9
2.7	.2	6	6.8	4.1	66.6	6.3	4.3
264 [7]	134 ₆0	64 509	55 980	65 478	14 853	190 103	448 033
55.8	2.4	11.2	22.6	27.2	9.3	18.2	7.5
8.2	.5	13.7	4.8	7.5	7.5	7.8	12
133 [7]	122 ₄8	99 659	49 916	65 587	23 267	220 994	531 070
56.6	2.1	17.3	20.2	27.2	14.6	21.2	8.9
8.4	.4	15.3	4.2	5.3	10	7.5	5.5
037 [7]	8 ₃2	33 094	16 454	24 185	4 480	26 648	43 831
1	.6	4	4	4.4	2.3	1.4	1

Included in figures
Refers to the publi
Including non-resid
rces: Population a
Accounts, Vol
Indicators. F
Financial Sta

November 1994

EMPLOYMENT OPPORTUNITIES

Economics Department, OECD

The Economics Department of the OECD offers challenging and rewarding opportunities to economists interested in applied policy analysis in an international environment. The Department's concerns extend across the entire field of economic policy analysis, both macroeconomic and microeconomic. Its main task is to provide, for discussion by committees of senior officials from Member countries, documents and papers dealing with current policy concerns. Within this programme of work, three major responsibilities are:

- to prepare regular surveys of the economies of individual Member countries;
- to issue full twice-yearly reviews of the economic situation and prospects of the OECD countries in the context of world economic trends;
- to analyse specific policy issues in a medium-term context for the OECD as a whole, and to a lesser extent for the non-OECD countries.

The documents prepared for these purposes, together with much of the Department's other economic work, appear in published form in the *OECD Economic Outlook, OECD Economic Surveys, OECD Economic Studies* and the Department's *Working Papers* series.

The Department maintains a world econometric model, INTERLINK, which plays an important role in the preparation of the policy analyses and twice-yearly projections. The availability of extensive cross-country data bases and good computer resources facilitates comparative empirical analysis, much of which is incorporated into the model.

The Department is made up of about 80 professional economists from a variety of backgrounds and Member countries. Most projects are carried out by small teams and last from four to eighteen months. Within the Department, ideas and points of view are widely discussed; there is a lively professional interchange, and all professional staff have the opportunity to contribute actively to the programme of work.

Skills the Economics Department is looking for:

a) Solid competence in using the tools of both microeconomic and macroeconomic theory to answer policy questions. Experience indicates that this normally requires the equivalent of a Ph.D. in economics or substantial relevant professional experience to compensate for a lower degree.

b) Solid knowledge of economic statistics and quantitative methods; this includes how to identify data, estimate structural relationships, apply basic techniques of time series analysis, and test hypotheses. It is essential to be able to interpret results sensibly in an economic policy context.

c) A keen interest in and extensive knowledge of policy issues, economic developments and their political/social contexts.

d) Interest and experience in analysing questions posed by policy-makers and presenting the results to them effectively and judiciously. Thus, work experience in government agencies or policy research institutions is an advantage.

e) The ability to write clearly, effectively, and to the point. The OECD is a bilingual organisation with French and English as the official languages. Candidates must have excellent knowledge of one of these languages, and some knowledge of the other. Knowledge of other languages might also be an advantage for certain posts.

f) For some posts, expertise in a particular area may be important, but a successful candidate is expected to be able to work on a broader range of topics relevant to the work of the Department. Thus, except in rare cases, the Department does not recruit narrow specialists.

g) The Department works on a tight time schedule with strict deadlines. Moreover, much of the work in the Department is carried out in small groups. Thus, the ability to work with other economists from a variety of cultural and professional backgrounds, to supervise junior staff, and to produce work on time is important.

General information

The salary for recruits depends on educational and professional background. Positions carry a basic salary from FF 305 700 or FF 377 208 for Administrators (economists) and from FF 438 348 for Principal Administrators (senior economists). This may be supplemented by expatriation and/or family allowances, depending on nationality, residence and family situation. Initial appointments are for a fixed term of two to three years.

Vacancies are open to candidates from OECD Member countries. The Organisation seeks to maintain an appropriate balance between female and male staff and among nationals from Member countries.

For further information on employment opportunities in the Economics Department, contact:

Administrative Unit
Economics Department
OECD
2, rue André-Pascal
75775 PARIS CEDEX 16
FRANCE

E-Mail: compte.esadmin@oecd.org

Applications citing "ECSUR", together with a detailed *curriculum vitae* in English or French, should be sent to the Head of Personnel at the above address.

MAIN SALES OUTLETS OF OECD PUBLICATIONS
PRINCIPAUX POINTS DE VENTE DES PUBLICATIONS DE L'OCDE

ARGENTINA – ARGENTINE
Carlos Hirsch S.R.L.
Galería Güemes, Florida 165, 4° Piso
1333 Buenos Aires   Tel. (1) 331.1787 y 331.2391
Telefax: (1) 331.1787

AUSTRALIA – AUSTRALIE
D.A. Information Services
648 Whitehorse Road, P.O.B 163
Mitcham, Victoria 3132   Tel. (03) 873.4411
Telefax: (03) 873.5679

AUSTRIA – AUTRICHE
Gerold & Co.
Graben 31
Wien I   Tel. (0222) 533.50.14
Telefax: (0222) 512.47.31.29

BELGIUM – BELGIQUE
Jean De Lannoy
Avenue du Roi 202 Koningslaan
B-1060 Bruxelles   Tel. (02) 538.51.69/538.08.41
Telefax: (02) 538.08.41

CANADA
Renouf Publishing Company Ltd.
1294 Algoma Road
Ottawa, ON K1B 3W8   Tel. (613) 741.4333
Telefax: (613) 741.5439
Stores:
61 Sparks Street
Ottawa, ON K1P 5R1   Tel. (613) 238.8985
211 Yonge Street
Toronto, ON M5B 1M4   Tel. (416) 363.3171
Telefax: (416)363.59.63

Les Éditions La Liberté Inc.
3020 Chemin Sainte-Foy
Sainte-Foy, PQ G1X 3V6   Tel. (418) 658.3763
Telefax: (418) 658.3763

Federal Publications Inc.
165 University Avenue, Suite 701
Toronto, ON M5H 3B8   Tel. (416) 860.1611
Telefax: (416) 860.1608

Les Publications Fédérales
1185 Université
Montréal, QC H3B 3A7   Tel. (514) 954.1633
Telefax: (514) 954.1635

CHINA – CHINE
China National Publications Import
Export Corporation (CNPIEC)
16 Gongti E. Road, Chaoyang District
P.O. Box 88 or 50
Beijing 100704 PR   Tel. (01) 506.6688
Telefax: (01) 506.3101

CHINESE TAIPEI – TAIPEI CHINOIS
Good Faith Worldwide Int'l. Co. Ltd.
9th Floor, No. 118, Sec. 2
Chung Hsiao E. Road
Taipei   Tel. (02) 391.7396/391.7397
Telefax: (02) 394.9176

CZECH REPUBLIC – RÉPUBLIQUE TCHÈQUE
Artia Pegas Press Ltd.
Narodni Trida 25
POB 825
111 21 Praha 1   Tel. 26.65.68
Telefax: 26.20.81

DENMARK – DANEMARK
Munksgaard Book and Subscription Service
35, Nørre Søgade, P.O. Box 2148
DK-1016 København K   Tel. (33) 12.85.70
Telefax: (33) 12.93.87

EGYPT – ÉGYPTE
Middle East Observer
41 Sherif Street
Cairo   Tel. 392.6919
Telefax: 360-6804

FINLAND – FINLANDE
Akateeminen Kirjakauppa
Keskuskatu 1, P.O. Box 128
00100 Helsinki
Subscription Services/Agence d'abonnements :
P.O. Box 23
00371 Helsinki   Tel. (358 0) 121 4416
Telefax: (358 0) 121.4450

FRANCE
OECD/OCDE
Mail Orders/Commandes par correspondance:
2, rue André-Pascal
75775 Paris Cedex 16   Tel. (33-1) 45.24.82.00
Telefax: (33-1) 49.10.42.76
Telex: 640048 OCDE
Internet: Compte.PUBSINQ @ oecd.org
Orders via Minitel, France only/
Commandes par Minitel, France exclusivement :
36 15 OCDE
OECD Bookshop/Librairie de l'OCDE :
33, rue Octave-Feuillet
75016 Paris   Tel. (33-1) 45.24.81.81
(33-1) 45.24.81.67
Documentation Française
29, quai Voltaire
75007 Paris   Tel. 40.15.70.00
Gibert Jeune (Droit-Économie)
6, place Saint-Michel
75006 Paris   Tel. 43.25.91.19
Librairie du Commerce International
10, avenue d'Iéna
75016 Paris   Tel. 40.73.34.60
Librairie Dunod
Université Paris-Dauphine
Place du Maréchal de Lattre de Tassigny
75016 Paris   Tel. (1) 44.05.40.13
Librairie Lavoisier
11, rue Lavoisier
75008 Paris   Tel. 42.65.39.95
Librairie L.G.D.J. - Montchrestien
20, rue Soufflot
75005 Paris   Tel. 46.33.89.85
Librairie des Sciences Politiques
30, rue Saint-Guillaume
75007 Paris   Tel. 45.48.36.02
P.U.F.
49, boulevard Saint-Michel
75005 Paris   Tel. 43.25.83.40
Librairie de l'Université
12a, rue Nazareth
13100 Aix-en-Provence   Tel. (16) 42.26.18.08
Documentation Française
165, rue Garibaldi
69003 Lyon   Tel. (16) 78.63.32.23
Librairie Decitre
29, place Bellecour
69002 Lyon   Tel. (16) 72.40.54.54
Librairie Sauramps
Le Triangle
34967 Montpellier Cedex 2   Tel. (16) 67.58.85.15
Tekefax: (16) 67.58.27.36

GERMANY – ALLEMAGNE
OECD Publications and Information Centre
August-Bebel-Allee 6
D-53175 Bonn   Tel. (0228) 959.120
Telefax: (0228) 959.12.17

GREECE – GRÈCE
Librairie Kauffmann
Mavrokordatou 9
106 78 Athens   Tel. (01) 32.55.321
Telefax: (01) 32.30.320

HONG-KONG
Swindon Book Co. Ltd.
Astoria Bldg. 3F
34 Ashley Road, Tsimshatsui
Kowloon, Hong Kong   Tel. 2376.2062
Telefax: 2376.0685

HUNGARY – HONGRIE
Euro Info Service
Margitsziget, Európa Ház
1138 Budapest   Tel. (1) 111.62.16
Telefax: (1) 111.60.61

ICELAND – ISLANDE
Mál Mog Menning
Laugavegi 18, Pósthólf 392
121 Reykjavik   Tel. (1) 552.4240
Telefax: (1) 562.3523

INDIA – INDE
Oxford Book and Stationery Co.
Scindia House
New Delhi 110001   Tel. (11) 331.5896/5308
Telefax: (11) 332.5993
17 Park Street
Calcutta 700016   Tel. 240832

INDONESIA – INDONÉSIE
Pdii-Lipi
P.O. Box 4298
Jakarta 12042   Tel. (21) 573.34.67
Telefax: (21) 573.34.67

IRELAND – IRLANDE
Government Supplies Agency
Publications Section
4/5 Harcourt Road
Dublin 2   Tel. 661.31.11
Telefax: 475.27.60

ISRAEL
Praedicta
5 Shatner Street
P.O. Box 34030
Jerusalem 91430   Tel. (2) 52.84.90/1/2
Telefax: (2) 52.84.93
R.O.Y. International
P.O. Box 13056
Tel Aviv 61130   Tel. (3) 546 1423
Telefax: (3) 546 1442
Palestinian Authority/Middle East:
INDEX Information Services
P.O.B. 19502
Jerusalem   Tel. (2) 27.12.19
Telefax: (2) 27.16.34

ITALY – ITALIE
Libreria Commissionaria Sansoni
Via Duca di Calabria 1/1
50125 Firenze   Tel. (055) 64.54.15
Telefax: (055) 64.12.57
Via Bartolini 29
20155 Milano   Tel. (02) 36.50.83
Editrice e Libreria Herder
Piazza Montecitorio 120
00186 Roma   Tel. 679.46.28
Telefax: 678.47.51
Libreria Hoepli
Via Hoepli 5
20121 Milano   Tel. (02) 86.54.46
Telefax: (02) 805.28.86
Libreria Scientifica
Dott. Lucio de Biasio 'Aeiou'
Via Coronelli, 6
20146 Milano   Tel. (02) 48.95.45.52
Telefax: (02) 48.95.45.48

JAPAN – JAPON
OECD Publications and Information Centre
Landic Akasaka Building
2-3-4 Akasaka, Minato-ku
Tokyo 107   Tel. (81.3) 3586.2016
Telefax: (81.3) 3584.7929

KOREA – CORÉE
Kyobo Book Centre Co. Ltd.
P.O. Box 1658, Kwang Hwa Moon
Seoul   Tel. 730.78.91
Telefax: 735.00.30

MALAYSIA – MALAISIE
University of Malaya Bookshop
University of Malaya
P.O. Box 1127, Jalan Pantai Baru
59700 Kuala Lumpur
Malaysia   Tel. 756.5000/756.5425
                                Telefax: 756.3246

MEXICO – MEXIQUE
Revistas y Periodicos Internacionales S.A. de C.V.
Florencia 57 - 1004
Mexico, D.F. 06600   Tel. 207.81.00
                                Telefax: 208.39.79

NETHERLANDS – PAYS-BAS
SDU Uitgeverij Plantijnstraat
Externe Fondsen
Postbus 20014
2500 EA's-Gravenhage   Tel. (070) 37.89.880
Voor bestellingen: Telefax: (070) 34.75.778

NEW ZEALAND
NOUVELLE-ZÉLANDE
GPLegislation Services
P.O. Box 12418
Thorndon, Wellington   Tel. (04) 496.5655
                            Telefax: (04) 496.5698

NORWAY – NORVÈGE
Narvesen Info Center – NIC
Bertrand Narvesens vei 2
P.O. Box 6125 Etterstad
0602 Oslo 6   Tel. (022) 57.33.00
                           Telefax: (022) 68.19.01

PAKISTAN
Mirza Book Agency
65 Shahrah Quaid-E-Azam
Lahore 54000   Tel. (42) 353.601
                           Telefax: (42) 231.730

PHILIPPINE – PHILIPPINES
International Book Center
5th Floor, Filipinas Life Bldg.
Ayala Avenue
Metro Manila   Tel. 81.96.76
                           Telex 23312 RHP PH

PORTUGAL
Livraria Portugal
Rua do Carmo 70-74
Apart. 2681
1200 Lisboa   Tel. (01) 347.49.82/5
                         Telefax: (01) 347.02.64

SINGAPORE – SINGAPOUR
Gower Asia Pacific Pte Ltd.
Golden Wheel Building
41, Kallang Pudding Road, No. 04-03
Singapore 1334   Tel. 741.5166
                           Telefax: 742.9356

SPAIN – ESPAGNE
Mundi-Prensa Libros S.A.
Castelló 37, Apartado 1223
Madrid 28001   Tel. (91) 431.33.99
                           Telefax: (91) 575.39.98

Libreria Internacional AEDOS
Consejo de Ciento 391
08009 – Barcelona   Tel. (93) 488.30.09
                           Telefax: (93) 487.76.59

Llibreria de la Generalitat
Palau Moja
Rambla dels Estudis, 118
08002 – Barcelona
        (Subscripcions) Tel. (93) 318.80.12
        (Publicacions) Tel. (93) 302.67.23
                           Telefax: (93) 412.18.54

SRI LANKA
Centre for Policy Research
c/o Colombo Agencies Ltd.
No. 300-304, Galle Road
Colombo 3   Tel. (1) 574240, 573551-2
                    Telefax: (1) 575394, 510711

SWEDEN – SUÈDE
Fritzes Customer Service
S–106 47 Stockholm   Tel. (08) 690.90.90
                           Telefax: (08) 20.50.21

Subscription Agency/Agence d'abonnements :
Wennergren-Williams Info AB
P.O. Box 1305
171 25 Solna   Tel. (08) 705.97.50
                           Telefax: (08) 27.00.71

SWITZERLAND – SUISSE
Maditec S.A. (Books and Periodicals - Livres
et périodiques)
Chemin des Palettes 4
Case postale 266
1020 Renens VD 1   Tel. (021) 635.08.65
                           Telefax: (021) 635.07.80

Librairie Payot S.A.
4, place Pépinet
CP 3212
1002 Lausanne   Tel. (021) 341.33.47
                           Telefax: (021) 341.33.45

Librairie Unilivres
6, rue de Candolle
1205 Genève   Tel. (022) 320.26.23
                           Telefax: (022) 329.73.18

Subscription Agency/Agence d'abonnements :
Dynapresse Marketing S.A.
38 avenue Vibert
1227 Carouge   Tel. (022) 308.07.89
                           Telefax: (022) 308.07.99

See also – Voir aussi :
OECD Publications and Information Centre
August-Bebel-Allee 6
D-53175 Bonn (Germany)   Tel. (0228) 959.120
                           Telefax: (0228) 959.12.17

THAILAND – THAÏLANDE
Suksit Siam Co. Ltd.
113, 115 Fuang Nakhon Rd.
Opp. Wat Rajbopith
Bangkok 10200   Tel. (662) 225.9531/2
                           Telefax: (662) 222.5188

TURKEY – TURQUIE
Kültür Yayinlari Is-Türk Ltd. Sti.
Atatürk Bulvari No. 191/Kat 13
Kavaklidere/Ankara   Tel. 428.11.40 Ext. 2458
Dolmabahce Cad. No. 29
Besiktas/Istanbul   Tel. (312) 260 7188
                           Telex: (312) 418 29 46

UNITED KINGDOM – ROYAUME-UNI
HMSO
Gen. enquiries   Tel. (171) 873 8496
Postal orders only:
P.O. Box 276, London SW8 5DT
Personal Callers HMSO Bookshop
49 High Holborn, London WC1V 6HB
                           Telefax: (171) 873 8416
Branches at: Belfast, Birmingham, Bristol,
Edinburgh, Manchester

UNITED STATES – ÉTATS-UNIS
OECD Publications and Information Center
2001 L Street N.W., Suite 650
Washington, D.C. 20036-4910 Tel. (202) 785.6323
                           Telefax: (202) 785.0350

VENEZUELA
Libreria del Este
Avda F. Miranda 52, Aptdo. 60337
Edificio Galipán
Caracas 106   Tel. 951.1705/951.2307/951.1297
                           Telegram: Libreste Caracas

Subscription to OECD periodicals may also be
placed through main subscription agencies.

Les abonnements aux publications périodiques de
l'OCDE peuvent être souscrits auprès des
principales agences d'abonnement.

Orders and inquiries from countries where Distribu-
tors have not yet been appointed should be sent to:
OECD Publications Service, 2 rue André-Pascal,
75775 Paris Cedex 16, France.

Les commandes provenant de pays où l'OCDE n'a
pas encore désigné de distributeur peuvent être
adressées à : OCDE, Service des Publications,
2, rue André-Pascal, 75775 Paris Cedex 16, France.

7-1995

PRINTED IN FRANCE

•

OECD PUBLICATIONS
2, rue André-Pascal
75775 PARIS CEDEX 16
No. 47871
(10 95 22 1) ISBN 92-64-14451-6
ISSN 0376-6438

•